becoming **unshakeable**

Dear Lisa,

May Knowledge, faith
and grace be your constant
companions.

Love,

Patti Montella

becoming
unshakeable

wisdom learned on the
journey to inner freedom

patti montella

LIONCREST
PUBLISHING

BECOMING UNSHAKEABLE
Wisdom Learned On The Journey To Inner Freedom

ISBN   978-1-5445-0431-5   *Hardcover*
        978-1-5445-0430-8   *Paperback*
        978-1-5445-0429-2   *Ebook*

Cover design by Marissa Rogers
Book design by John van der Woude

For my beloved Gurudev

contents

Every moment that you spend here, in this place, just know that you are in a Divine place. You are in the Divine space. Know that you are on this planet for a very unique and big purpose, not just to eat, sleep and talk. You are here for a greater cause. Just remember that.

Let us resolve to be unshakeable within and move towards a better world.

Time changes people but there are people who change the time.

May you be one of them.

—His Holiness Sri Sri Ravi Shankar

close a window;
open a door

James lay in the hospital bed, his eyes staring into some void. He could no longer see me or his other friends and family in the room. Moments later, for the first time, I witnessed the transformation of someone moving from this space to that space. Suddenly, my consciousness was lifted up to another dimension, which is now so obvious to me and so much a part of my daily reality, yet my eyes had been shut to it up until that point. The experience of James's death changed everything I thought I knew about life. Unanswered questions raced through my mind. I wondered why I'd never thought about them before.

The staff, who had been so cruel when we had first checked James in as the hospital's first AIDS patient, were crying uncontrollably, as was his father, who after years of estrangement had come to be by James's side. With one final breath, his only son—so full of unconditional love and who had just turned twenty-four years old—was gone. Standing against the cold gray hospital wall as though it could somehow hold me up, I watched his lifeless body being wheeled away. In that moment, I realized how easily I'd taken life for granted.

Just a few months earlier, I was the one who had brought James to the hospital the day he received the crushing blow of his diagnosis, and—along with his partner—served as his caregiver from that moment until the day he died. I was in my early thirties, and the AIDS epidemic of the 1990s was sweeping the nation. James was but one of many dear friends who would lose their lives to the disease.

James's passing came on the heels of the unraveling of my marriage and on the precipice of major career changes. Disillusioned to discover that the "perfect" life, which I'd worked so hard to create, left me empty and miserable inside, I felt like a part of myself had also died that day. It was a time of great uncertainty.

My faith—in myself, in the good of society, and in the presence of a Divine Power to guide and protect us—was deeply shaken. I had reached a tipping point. The experience launched me on a quest to discover the truth about life, before it all came to an end.

I walked out of the hospital in silence, passing a toddler, who was gleefully running away from her mother. Instinctively, the mother reached out and grabbed the child's hand—leading her to safety. I vaguely remembered my own mother doing the same for me, the first time I ran away to explore on my own.

What follows is an accounting of some of the twists, turns, and hurdles I encountered on my journey, along with the astounding spiritual revelations that unveiled themselves along the way. There were many times—like that of laying twenty-four-year-old James to rest—when my faith on the path was shaken to the core. What I now know in hindsight is that those were the precise moments that awakened me to the part of myself that is unshakeable.

This is the path that I chose. It is not the only one, nor is it cut out for everyone, and it was undoubtedly made more difficult from the obstacles I placed in my own way. In the overcoming of these obstacles, I have discovered an inner self-reliance that is independent of anyone or anything outside the self; a reliable pathway back home to the love, joy, and peace we all are at our core.

It is my sincere honor to share this wisdom with you, and it is my greatest hope that in the sharing, your path to the discovery of your own inner beauty and divinity will be made that much lighter and easier.

Patti Montella
Boone, North Carolina, Spring, 2019

the foundation **is laid**

I was born into a devout and loving Catholic family, the third of four girls. From the get-go, I was happy, sensitive, and fiercely independent. My mother would tell you I wasn't an easy child to raise, adding that the fact that I had a good heart made it all possible. After living with my grandparents for a little while in the city of Buffalo, my parents bought a home in the suburbs. Almost all of the neighborhood kids were also Catholic, which meant that once a week yellow school buses lined up at our elementary school to take us to church for religion instruction classes. I never enjoyed religious training and envied the non-Catholics who got to go home early to play.

Mom and Dad moved from Florida to Buffalo, New York, just after Dad left his career with the U.S. Marine Corps. At the time, Mom was pregnant with me—baby number three. My father began his career as a diesel mechanic with a national trucking firm the same day that I arrived. He was up and out the door early for work every morning and home every evening for dinner. Mom was a superb homemaker as well as an accomplished artist. When I was in high school, she went to work part-time and was always home by the time we returned from school.

My father is a wise man. Along with teaching me how to keep a sense of humor, and to demand respect, he taught me patience, how to throw a baseball and how to dance. Mom is the ultimate caretaker in every way. She gave me a strong foundation of faith, watched over my studies, and as a talented vocalist, she made sure that I learned a musical instrument and developed an appreciation for the arts.

Raising four girls is an expensive venture, so in order to provide extras, my parents learned how to build and repair just about anything. Together, they remodeled our basement into a large playroom, along with a laundry room and tool shop. I played pool in that basement, learned the latest dance steps, and kissed my first boyfriend. Dad often took on a second job every year, just to make sure we had everything we could ever want for Christmas—an important holiday in our family, both religiously and as a family celebration. While winter can be harsh in upstate New York, it offers all kinds of fun in the snow. My sisters and I built snow forts, ice-skated, sledded, and had the occasional neighborhood snowball fight.

Our home held a lot of love, laughter, and music, and as we grew older, our family discussed current events over the dinner table. No doubt there were fights between us sisters, but we enjoyed one another's company and always had one another's back. Overall, I enjoyed a pretty happy and healthy childhood.

Patti at 6 years old.

When I turned sixteen, like my sisters before me, I started working part-time at a local Greek diner in our neighborhood, in order to save up for my first car and college. My own family frequented the diner, along with people from every walk of life; from truckers, school teachers, and students, to business and community leaders, sports celebrities, and even the occasional mobster! First generation Americans of European descent ran most of the businesses in the same shopping plaza where the diner was located. The Greeks who operated the diner were like family to us, and we joked and laughed with the barbers from Italy next door. Whenever I visited the bakery owned by a family from Poland, they always gave me something sweet along with a big smile. The tapestry of people and cultures in my small neighborhood not only nurtured a healthy sense of belonging with people from all backgrounds, it also helped to fuel my sense of adventure for travel.

Life moved along in a fairly normal fashion, until an inner restlessness to find out the truth about life began rising like a smoldering volcano within me when I was sixteen years old. Around this time, like most teenagers, I started rebelling. And, like a lot of teenagers at the time in the USA, I experimented with things that aren't good for the body or mind, including sneaking out to drink bottles of cheap wine and hanging out with people my parents never would have approved of. My parents are very smart, and because they went the distance to keep tabs on me, more often than not, I was caught red-handed. "You can't con a con-artist," my father used to tell me, just before handing out a punishment. I spent more time being grounded during high school than any other teenager I knew—including all my sisters.

The families of my best friends in high school attended the same church as our family, and our parents were friendly with them. We went to school together, rode bikes and played together, and once we started driving, we sneaked out together. One Saturday evening, three of us conspired to tell our parents we were going to the movies when we were actually going to a party. My boyfriend's older brother was hosting it while his parents were out for the night.

My parents put the pieces of our lie together and within a few hours, to my complete embarrassment, my father showed up at the party in the green family station wagon. There were people openly partying on the lawn along with motorcycles and a lot of people much older than my friends and me. My father honked the horn so loud that no one could miss it when he shouted, "I am Patti Montella's father. Where is my daughter?!" I wanted to crawl under that house from embarrassment but had no choice but to climb into the back seat of that car along with my two best friends. After this scene, I never snuck out of the house again.

Our family attended church together every Sunday, followed by a ride in the country and a stop for some sort of treat. By the time my sisters and I were teenagers, all we wanted to listen to was rock music and hang out with our friends, but still my parents insisted and off we went. The long country drives got pretty interesting every now and then when my maternal grandmother, who had a great interest in metaphysics, went with us to visit Lilydale, a famous summer resort for psychics.

I had my first of many psychic "readings" when I was just sixteen and was shocked when the tiny old woman accurately described exactly what I'd been thinking and doing just the day before. She also gave me a message from my deceased grandfather. This early exposure to another dimension of life made a lasting impression.

Meanwhile, my teenage rebellion grew stronger by the day. One Sunday, just as the family was getting ready to go to church, I informed my father that I would not be joining the family. "How do I know what I've been told and have read about Jesus is true? I want to find out the truth for myself, in my own way," I said with my hands on my hips and an unmistakable air of defiance.

This was the first, but not the last time, my very patient father slowly and very clearly let me know, in no uncertain terms, that as long as I lived in his house, I would follow his rules. Angry and defeated, I dramatically burst into tears, stormed out of the house and into the car. When the priest invited our family to bring up the communion gifts during mass, it was all I could do to keep my composure walking up to the altar while hot tears of frustration fell from my eyes. That day, I became more resolved than ever before to find out the truth about life, on my own terms, as soon as I was old enough to live on my own.

I grew up during the 1960s and '70s, which represented a time of great revolution in the United States. The country was torn apart by the Vietnam War. The Cold War between the USA and Russia was also taking place, which meant regular "Duck and Cover" drills in school, in case of a possible nuclear attack. Just like the time we live in now, there was a lot of fear to go around, even without a twenty-four-hour news cycle.

Race-related riots began just after I was born. The year President John F. Kennedy proposed the legislation that would eventually become the Civil Rights Act, I was about to enter kindergarten. He was assassinated that fall. The day of JFK's funeral, my mother called me in from playing, to respectfully watch the funeral procession.

The Vietnam War started a few years before I was born and by the time it ended, I was a sophomore in high school. I was usually in bed before the nightly news on a school night, but now and then I caught some images of the fighting overseas, along with the student protests at home and flag-draped coffins of young men returning to the USA. So, in spite of my age, I was very much aware of what was happening abroad and in our country.

Along with student protests at universities across the country over the Vietnam War, riots erupted in 1968, sparked by the assassination of Reverend Martin Luther King, Jr., followed by Senator Robert F. Kennedy. I was ten years old at the time, and while I couldn't fully understand the magnitude of what was happening, the sense of fear in the country was palpable. My elementary school teacher took it upon herself to teach us folk songs of peace, including, "If I Had a Hammer..." which we sang with all our hearts.

As the country continued to shift and evolve, so did our family. I don't know how my parents managed it, but every summer we were fortunate to go on some kind of vacation, whether it was to Connecticut to visit my dad's family who lived near the beach, or now and then to a vacation destination along the East Coast.

Everyone in my family has a good sense of humor, with my father getting the award as head comic. I wasn't even old enough to attend school when I discovered how good it felt to make people laugh. Being the third of four girls meant I wore a lot of hand-me-downs, which more often than not, were too big for me. One of my "first comedy acts" was hiding in the hallway closet and swinging the door open as fast as possible, while wiggling my whole body in order to make my pajama bottoms fall down. My sisters broke into gales of laughter every single time. Variety shows were popular while I was growing up; I probably got the idea from a skit I'd seen. Two of my favorite shows growing up were *The Red Skelton Show* (a well-known comic) and *I Love Lucy*.

Along with comedy, my sisters and I also imitated Catholic church services. We would set up a makeshift altar in our bedroom. Perhaps in imitating sacred rituals, I was foreshadowing a life to come. My older sister was usually the priest, and the rest of us were nuns or parishioners receiving Holy Communion. We held funerals for our goldfish, turtles and other creatures, burying them in a box outside in our mother's garden.

First communion.

I was raised to be patriotic and grew up at a time when schoolchildren pledged allegiance to the flag before starting the day. As a Marine, my father led by example when it came to honor and duty for our country. One summer, during a parade at a festival, I started making a few jokes with my sister about the ongoing number of flags in the parade. Out of the corner of his eye, my father caught us being disrespectful. The next thing I knew he was instructing us both to stand at attention and to salute every single flag that passed by, until the entire parade was over. We had no choice but to put our hands to our heads for the next hour whether it was the 4 H Club flag, a simple flag tucked into the harness of a horse, or a large American flag. There turned out to be fifty flags in all, and by the time we were allowed to lower our now sore arms, we made a pact to never joke about any flag again!

My parents have a high work ethic, a strong faith in God, and a great sense of service toward others. They regularly instilled these values, along with a sense of gratitude, in all of us girls, which also paved the way for my future in a life of service. Early on, they helped to kindle a deep compassion within me to care for those who are less fortunate. Along with stretching a helping hand to anyone who needed it, every now and then, they would take us for a drive out of our serene suburb with its green manicured lawns and into the big city. Four girls can create a lot of noise, but our car quickly became silent as we wound our way through some of the poorest areas of the city. I'll never forget images of kids who lived in what were called "the projects," playing in the dirt where grass hadn't grown for many years. My heart sank when we passed the city orphanage that loomed in the dark of night, looking more like a haunted house than a place that cared for children. It's my earliest memory of feeling grateful for what we had and compassion toward others who were less fortunate.

On our way to Disney World the year it opened, my parents went out of their way to take us through the outskirts of the Deep South. We passed by families living in poverty in simple shacks made out of tar paper. My eyes popped open wide at the sight of prisoners linked together with ankle shackles and heavy iron balls as they worked in the heat of the fields. I learned that these were called prison "chain-gangs," a cruel system popular in the South at the time.

I was the kid who always asked questions and raised my hand to volunteer. By fourteen, I was a volunteer with our church youth group, at seventeen, I was the youth representative for our city council and by eighteen, I was volunteering at a Veterans Hospital after seeing a movie about the Vietnam War. I was interested in just about everything, and volunteering was a great way to contribute, to learn new things and to meet all kinds of interesting people.

Unlike today, attending college wasn't quite as common when I graduated high school in 1976. My parents never pressured me in any direction; they only wanted to see me happy with whatever path I chose. The idea of working while attending college didn't resonate with me, and I had a burning desire to see the world. So rather than becoming a journalist, I started applying to the airlines, my second career choice.

My career with American Airlines and the SABRE Corporation—leaders in the airline and travel technology industry—spanned twenty years. I was just twenty years old when I began six weeks of grueling training at American's Training Academy located just outside of Dallas, Texas. I started at the bottom rung of the corporate ladder as a reservation agent, and by the time I left the company, I was an executive in the field of travel technology, where I helped to launch several companies and global products.

After completing training, I had one weekend to return home, pack up my few belongings, and move to Hartford, Connecticut, in time to begin my job the following Monday morning. To fund the move, I had no choice but to sell my precious and very cool car. Everyone in my life seemed to be excited for me; people at the diner gifted me with a new suitcase and some money to begin my journey. Mom packed me up, while Dad arranged for a trucker at his company to bring

American Airlines.

my things to Connecticut on his next trip. There was no time to find a place to live in just one weekend, so the mother of a friend from my training class drove from New York and rented each of us a studio apartment in downtown Hartford.

Mom and Dad.

Suitcases in hand, I walked out of the security and warmth of my family and into the next chapter of life. Ironically, I was the kid who was always scared of "things that go bump in the night," so no one was happier than I was to discover that several friends from my training class had also moved into the same rundown building on Asylum Avenue—a street that proved to live up to its name.

I had zero knowledge of how to live on my own when I started out. I didn't know the first thing about cooking, and so, as a joke, my friends created a cookbook that included how to boil water and make toast. I'd never even washed or ironed my own clothes. Now that I didn't own a car, I had to take a bus or walk—everywhere. I worked the night shift, and living downtown meant I had to learn things like how to cross the street back and forth, in order to avoid the prostitutes and drunks who lingered about at night. Still, it was thrilling to finally be on my own and making my own decisions.

My father's family lived just an hour away on Long Island Sound, which made living in Connecticut on my own and without a car a little easier. Whenever possible, I took the train to spend the weekend with my aunts or to hang out with my cousins.

A lot of things happened during my first year on my own that chipped away at my innocence and naivete. Within a month or so of starting my job, one of American's jumbo jets crashed in Chicago and many people died. I was on duty that day. As a new reservation agent, I handled many of the heart-wrenching calls from family who were searching for their loved ones, who had perished. Unfortunately, it was not the first airplane crash I would face in my career with the airline.

I'd been dating a great guy when I joined the airline industry and moved away from home. He expected that we would eventually marry, but at that point in my life, I had no intention of being tied down. I'd already turned down another marriage proposal from someone else a year earlier. He, too, was a wonderful guy, but I was eager to take in all that life had to offer, especially since I now worked for an international airline with all kinds of flight benefits.

Excited that my sister and her husband were coming for a visit a few months after I moved in, I bought flowers and filled the fridge with all the foods they would enjoy. We had a nice weekend together, but in spite of my sincere attempts, there was no masking my dismal and unsafe living situation—which was all I could afford on $1.97 an hour. They sat me down just before leaving and made me promise to move out before my parents ever saw the place. Nine months after I started my career with American Airlines, I transferred to the company's headquarters, in Dallas, Texas, which quickly kicked off a whole new phase of life.

"You've always marched to the beat of your own drum," my parents used to say. And while they haven't always agreed with my lifestyle choices, especially when I left a successful business career to follow a Guru from India around the world—they laid the foundation for the work I would eventually dedicate my life to. I just had a few more life lessons, along with some twists and turns to navigate, before that time would arrive.

I was twenty-three years old when I fell in love with a man eleven years my senior. He was of Mexican heritage, worked for the same company, and had served in Vietnam. While he was charming, funny, and attentive, he also had an air about him that beckoned me to be careful. When we first met, I was dating an engineering student from Greece and we were entertaining the idea of marriage.

My future husband pursued me for another year, and when my other relationship ended, I finally relented. After one long conversation, I fell in love. "What? Is this the same man you said was too old for you and you weren't certain about?" asked my very surprised mother. In spite of my parents' concern over marrying him, along with my own doubts, we tied the knot surrounded by friends and family and a chorus of Mariachis.

My career was on the upswing; however, married life was a struggle almost from the start. I knew when we married that he drank too much, but like many young women, I was naïve enough to think our love was enough to change the situation.

We never spoke about what we expected out of marriage, and I assumed it would reflect the example set by my parents, who loved and respected one another. However, my husband's early experiences were much different. He had grown up in a Texas border town, his mother did shift work, and his father was out of the picture from the start. Very quickly, I was living in two worlds; by day, I was a successful corporate executive, and at night, I was a miserable housewife. Our home was regularly filled with people who drank, did drugs and stayed up late into the night with my husband, including his friends, who were players in Texas politics at the time. Make no mistake, I did my fair share of partying, but the difference between us was that I could stop—he couldn't. I was so ashamed of how my life was unraveling, that over time I began isolating myself more and more from my family and friends.

With an abundance of disposable income, expensive cars, and the ability to travel wherever and whenever we wanted, to the outside world, it looked like we had it all. But the truth was that our relationship was toxic, he was crashing car after car while drinking, and no amount of material comfort could diminish the misery in our lives. We did love one another, but it was a distorted form of love between an alcoholic and a codependent. We tried going to church together and then to marriage counseling in an attempt to save what was left of our relationship, but I knew that unless he gave up the alcohol, it was never going to work. When, during our first couple's session, our marriage counselor whispered into my ear, "Divorce him as fast as you can!" it was clear we had come to the end of the road.

The toll of an unhealthy marriage, combined with a high-stress career, eventually impacted my health. During a particularly difficult time, my family physician sat me down for a serious talk. "Patti, stress will eventually have its way with you. If you have a strong body, it will attack your mind. You have a strong mind, so it's attacking your body. If you continue in this way, you will lose your health altogether." My husband and I stayed together a total of four years until I realized that nothing was going to change unless I changed. I'd tried leaving him a few times but had returned for one reason or another.

I finally took action one weekend, when he once again went missing for days, to parts unknown. Packing whatever I could fit into two suitcases, I hugged the dog, walked out for good, and moved in with a friend. The first year on my own was the hardest, but with the help of good friends, I eventually moved into my own place, settled the divorce, and moved forward.

After I was settled, I started taking night classes at the local community college and eventually transferred to a larger university. The idea of becoming a journalist was still nagging at me, and the thought of changing my career along with everything else was enticing. The travel technology industry was booming at the time, and my company was at the forefront of it. Eventually, simultaneously juggling classes with an intense travel schedule became too much, and I let college go.

The following year, my ex-husband checked himself into a rehabilitation center. With no friends or family to help him through it, I acted as a witness to help him help himself. As he was being taken to his room, one of the counselors turned to me and surprised me when he asked, "And you? What are you doing to address your own feelings?" "*Feelings?* I thought to myself...I don't have any feelings." I could not have been more clueless about myself. I was supporting his rehabilitation process in order to understand why I'd chosen to marry an alcoholic. I attended a few Al-Anon meetings and started reading books about codependence, which took me on a powerful path of self-discovery. In time, he got better and so did I, and we went our separate ways.

By this time, I was longing to stop thinking about myself and to get back to what had always given me the greatest joy in life—volunteering.

At that time, the Fort Worth, Texas, chapter of The Special Olympics—the world's largest sports organization for children and adults with intellectual disabilities—was looking for volunteers. I eagerly signed up and in the first meeting, I knew I was back where I belonged. My first assignment was a big challenge. I was tasked with recruiting and organizing 1,500 volunteers to support 3,000 athletes during our Spring Games event at a local university. I enjoyed every minute of service to TSO and remained a dedicated volunteer for more than fifteen years.

Polo.

During a fundraiser for another nonprofit the following year, a friend encouraged me to bid on an unusual item during the Silent Auction. I'd ridden horses since I was a teenager, and a new Polo Club was offering lessons at a greatly reduced rate. My friend reasoned that playing polo would provide a way to spend time around horses—and, she added, "It's a great way to meet wealthy men." Nobody was more shocked than I was when I won the bid.

For the next several years, I forgot about romance and enjoyed polo scrimmages on the weekends, both at home and at a Caribbean resort I liked to frequent. I played hard and worked hard, continuing my volunteer service along with everything that comes with a demanding corporate career. My younger sister was also advancing her career in the country music industry at the time and was encouraging me to step out socially more. I started hanging out with celebrities from the Nashville music scene and had a great time.

My home was now peaceful, I enjoyed the company of good friends and family along with volunteer work, and I was at the top of my career—still, something was missing from my life.

Unsure of what it was that was calling me from within, I joined a metaphysical group, but when it didn't offer any depth of understanding into the universal truths about life that I was looking for, I left within a year. When a friend, who was deeply involved in Native American traditions invited me to some programs, I went. I connected with the wisdom of that path, but after one awkward sweat lodge, I moved on. When I was eventually introduced to the book, A Course in Miracles, something familiar began stirring deep within me, and I joined a study group in Dallas.

Years earlier, just as my marriage was ending, I'd started suffering from migraine headaches, which continued for years and eventually reduced my quality of life. Nothing the allopathic doctors prescribed alleviated the pain, nor did the drugs stop the debilitating cycle of cluster migraines that showed up every other month. One day at the office, I heard my inner voice (the one we all have but don't always listen to) whispering, "You don't breathe enough." I stopped what I was doing and took notice of the rhythm of my breath, something I never did before unless I was out of breath. I noticed that I was holding my breath and started taking long, slow deep breaths in and out. Within minutes, my whole body relaxed and the intensity of the migraine lessened. From then on, whenever I felt the stirrings of a headache, I went out to my car so that I could close my eyes, and take as many long, slow deep breaths as it took for the migraine to diminish altogether.

Simultaneously, I was hatching a plan to leave the corporate life in order to start my own business in Colorado. I'd been skiing there for years, and the weather and lifestyle agreed with me—as did the mountains. The day my doctor recommended I move out of state to get away from the allergies was the same day that a sales position opened up in Denver for the first time in fourteen years. I decided it was time to downgrade my position with the company in order to upgrade my quality of life. Little did I know just how much my life was about to change and that the Divine, a higher power, was orchestrating the whole thing.

when the student is ready,
the master appears

Starting over in a new state, without the support of friends or family, took courage. While the job was a downgrade financially, it came with a lot of lifestyle bonuses. I was living in a vacation destination with a healthier climate. I was blessed with a good income, healthcare, and access to all the ski passes I could ever want. I rented a small house in the center of the city, volunteered with a few organizations, and got to work.

Life was humming along pretty nicely with only one glitch. It turned out that the man who hired me for the job didn't like me at all. I was a woman, and I was bold and smart—three strikes in his book. Still, I liked the work and the dynamism of the job and had a feeling I'd made the right move. To validate that decision, a few months later, what started out as a normal business day changed my life forever.

September 21, 1995
"A new era for all mankind began today where more faith and dedication will dawn. The devas and subtle beings are creating more faith in people everywhere, and the emphasis is now on matter to spirit; moving from the material to the spiritual.

"In India there is an upsurge in spiritual awareness such that people who have not been to temple for years are now flocking to temples everywhere. It has been seen that the raw milk that has been placed in front of the statue of Ganesh (deity who removes obstacles and brings prosperity) has disappeared."

—*Sri Sri Ravi Shankar*

I was in Boulder one afternoon, meeting with a client. Just before leaving, I stopped to introduce myself to Marie, one of the managers, and within seconds of sitting down in her office, a flyer fell off of her desk. "This has been falling off of my desk all day...I think it's for you," she said, handing me a piece of paper promoting something called The Healing Breath Workshop with the Art of Living Foundation.

I had already had a little introduction to the power of my own breath in relieving migraines, so I agreed to take the workshop with her, on the spot.

Walking up to a charming home in the heart of Boulder where the course was taking place, both Marie and I started having second thoughts. "I don't know if this is the right move," she said. "We just met and neither of us knows anything about this workshop, not really. What if you don't like it?" she asked, full of apprehension. We stood under the light of a streetlamp, weighing our options, when suddenly three deer walked out of the woods, stopped and stared at us. The deer is the Native American totem that represents intuition and the ability to move through life and obstacles with grace. We both knew their arrival was an auspicious sign, so we knocked on the door and walked in. Closing the door behind me to keep the chill out of the warm kitchen, I turned to meet Jane, who owned the home the workshop was taking place in. Her million dollar smile made the cozy kitchen even warmer, as did her welcome. "I'm David," said a friendly man, while handing me a course application. "I'll be your teacher."

Immediately noticing a laid-back sense of ease and friendliness about him, I relaxed. "Do you know anything about this course?" he asked with a big smile. "It's about breathing. That's all I know," I said, shrugging my shoulders. "Very good!" he remarked, taking me into the living room where the course was about to begin.

The small group of students gathered was an eclectic mix of people including business professionals, hippies, professors, people out of work and homemakers. The cynical part of my nature began stirring with the first awkward ice-breaker.

During a break, I struck up a conversation with a somewhat odd and deeply introspective man sitting beside me, and asked him what he did for a living. I was already beginning to feel the workshop might not be the right fit for me, when he replied, "I'm depressed." I started thinking in earnest about how to make my exit.

David returned to continue teaching and his presence was so peaceful and disarming that I relaxed again. After learning just a few breathing techniques, I was surprised at how refreshed I felt and that my normally busy mind was actually quiet. Still, I wasn't sure if I wanted to return the next day and neither was Marie. Before the evening ended, David told us a little bit about the *Sudarshan Kriya*™ breathing technique that we would learn the following day. "This is the cornerstone of the Healing Breath workshop and you don't want to miss it." The conviction in his voice and the sense of mystery around the technique was just enough to get me to agree to show up.

The next morning, restless and curious, I struggled to keep my eyes closed through the breathing processes when we began. But before I knew it, my body was completely relaxed along with my mind. A few minutes into the *Sudarshan Kriya* breathing technique I felt like I was in a bubble of peace, the likes of which I'd never known.

When it was over, we were invited to share our experience. One by one, everyone shared the same: they all felt lighter, happier, and at peace, as did I. One man said he hadn't felt so much energy in years and that he thought he could run a marathon!

It was difficult to express all that I experienced. What I was able to share was that after a painful marriage and divorce, followed by my friend's long illness and death, it felt as though my heart had a hole in it. But now, I literally felt as though some healing had taken place, and the hole was now filled with love. So while I didn't understand how breathing in rhythms created such a powerful and unique experience of being free, I was eager to repeat it.

In spite of putting up a strong outward façade, I'd never told anyone how alone I'd felt during those difficult years surrounding my divorce. And this is why I was so surprised by my experience on day two of the *Sudarshan Kriya*. I had a powerful vision and heard a voice from far away that said, "Patti, we're holding your hands. Be patient, we're still building your new life for you. We're right here and always have been."

The realization that I was not walking alone on this earth; that there was a higher power, a Divine presence, with me all the time, brought me to tears. The expansion I experienced was out of this world, and I silently created an intention to share this workshop with everyone I met.

When we were done, the teacher announced that an informative video about Sri Sri Ravi Shankar, who conceived the *Sudarshan Kriya* practice, would play during our break if we'd like to watch it. While everyone got up for lunch, I stayed back to watch the video playing on the tiny television sitting on the fireplace hearth. A man from India with long black hair and big brown eyes who exuded the deepest sense of peace was giving a discourse on *Patanjali's Yoga Sutras*, an ancient spiritual text on the philosophy of yoga.

Knowledge of the breath improves the quality of life.

Within the breath is the secret of life. Breath is the link between our body, spirit and mind. Our breath is linked to our emotions and for every emotion, there is a particular rhythm in the breath. If we understand the rhythm of our breath, we are able to have a say over our mind. We can win over any negative emotions such as fear, anxiety, greed or jealousy, and are able to smile more from our heart.

—Sri Sri Ravi Shankar

The video began and I heard him say, *"Sometimes it is not just physical illness but mental and emotional illness too that need to be dealt with. Anger, lust, greed, jealousy, etc. How does one get rid of all these impurities? What is the formula?"* I was captivated by his powerful presence to such an extent that I couldn't move or take my eyes off of him. In a matter of seconds, the words he was speaking went into the background and my heart became so full I thought it would burst. Time seemed to stand still. His message was so universal, so inclusive, and he exuded such unconditional love that I knew my search was finally over; I was home.

I took my teacher's recommendation to commit to a daily practice of the breathing techniques I'd just learned for forty days. I also went from being a skeptic on the first night of the course to volunteering to help David organize a wisdom series in Denver. Intuitively, I felt that Sri Sri (Gurudev) was the "real deal," and I intended to soak up any and every bit of wisdom he had to share.

I'd suffered from allergies my entire life, but after the Healing Breath Workshop (now called the Happiness Program) I was free of all allergy symptoms as well as migraines. After getting my doctor's okay, I dumped all my medicines into the garbage without looking back. I started attending *satsang* (gatherings in the company of truth) where I could sink back into the bliss of the longer breathing meditation technique that I'd enjoyed on the course.

I don't know what I expected would happen spiritually during the forty-day commitment phase, but I didn't get any magical, mystical experiences. What I did notice was what happened to me the first time I missed my daily *sādhanā* (spiritual practices). The alarm clock went off as usual, but the entire day I felt like I was walking in mud— backward. I was sluggish, people seemed to annoy me more than usual, and I struggled to keep my focus in the late afternoon after a series of meetings.

After a few months, I had the same experience anytime I missed my daily practice. Eventually, I realized that an extra thirty minutes of sleep, instead of getting up to breathe and meditate, only made the day more difficult to get through.

Daily *sādhanā* was the one constant that helped me to steady my mind and release pent-up stress along with a host of negative emotions including fear about keeping my job. Around the same time that I began attending Gurudev's discourse on *Patanjali Yoga Sutras*, I was also delving into other ancient spiritual texts as well, including *Narada Bhakti Sutras* (aphorisms of love) and the *Ashtavakra Gita*, the blueprint to liberation.

'Su' means proper, 'darshan' means vision, and 'Kriya' is a purifying practice. The Sudarshan Kriya is therefore a purifying practice, whereby one receives a proper vision of one's true self. This unique breathing practice is a potent energizer. The breath connects the body and mind. Just as emotions affect our patterns of breathing, we can bring about changes in our mental and behavioral patterns by altering the rhythms of our breath. It flushes our anger, anxiety and worry, leaving the mind completely relaxed and energized. And when we feel good about ourselves, love flows naturally in all our relationships with others.
—Sri Sri Ravi Shankar

Each one offered immense knowledge into the science of the mind and emotions and how to break free of patterns and impressions that didn't serve my highest good. In no time at all, I noticed that I was becoming much more aware and clear in my mind. Instead of waking up a few times a night, I was sleeping better and had more energy, not only at the job but on my time off as well. After a few months, I began noticing that I wasn't getting as upset as I used to when my boss or someone else said something irritating. I felt more self-confident and, more often than not, found that I was responding, instead of reacting, to difficult people and situations.

I also seemed to be getting more done in less time, with fewer mistakes since taking the program and regularly practicing the techniques. In the past, preparing for our quarterly sales presentation was a huge stress, and I would be up until 3:00 a.m. just before catching a 7:00 a.m. flight. But now, I was able to get a good night's sleep and felt much more rested for the big presentation. Even my highly critical boss noticed a difference, and the next time I gave a sales presentation, he praised me instead of finding fault. The interesting thing about it was my numbers hadn't changed at all—the only thing that had shifted was within me.

So when I learned that the Art of Living Foundation was offering a silent meditation retreat in the mountains, I immediately signed up. Since everything I'd experienced so far on this path had brought more ease into my life, I wanted to see what the advanced program offered.

But within days of signing up, the resistance in my own mind started kicking in. First, I was told there would be no talking after the first day, and no reading, television or journaling. My friends started taking bets on how long it would take me to crack! I wasn't vegetarian at the time, and when I heard that the menu was "light-vegetarian," I packed snacks just in case I got hungry.

The first day of the course, up in the beautiful Rocky Mountains just outside of Colorado Springs, was easy enough and I enjoyed the privacy of my own cabin in the woods. The next morning I rose very early, along with everyone else, to enjoy a sunrise yoga and meditation session. Chuckling to myself over breakfast, I popped one of the bagels I'd packed, into the toaster before doing some *Seva* (service) and taking a walk. It all seemed quite peaceful and easy, until the afternoon.

By the third meditation that day, my bottom hurt from sitting and I was starting to get bored. I snuck in a few cookies during the break just before we were put into silence. I groaned aloud when we sat for more meditation, counting the hours until dinner, along with the birds in the trees outside.

I regretted not bringing my own car to the course, so that I could at least go to town to get a cup of coffee. During the evening *satsang*, a fellow corporate road-warrior passed me a note saying that she was jealous of how deep I was in every meditation. I just smiled before returning to my cabin, where the only sound was the clock ticking and the fire crackling in the wood stove. Before I knew it, the alarm was ringing at 6:00 a.m. sharp and it was time for another morning yoga and meditation session. During lunch, the same friend slipped me another note that read: "I'm not jealous anymore. You're not meditating; you're sleeping. Get rid of the snacks."

She was right; the extra food was making me sleepy. To get it out of my system, I went for a long walk, all the while contemplating my options for leaving the course. I was restless sitting for so long and wanted to do anything but sit and meditate any more. That afternoon the teacher played a knowledge video with Gurudev. As soon as it began, I felt as though he was speaking right to me.

"A commitment can only be felt when it oversteps convenience. If you just go on your convenience, your commitment falls apart causing more inconvenience! If you keep dropping your commitment because it is inconvenient, can you be comfortable? Often, what is convenient does not bring comfort but gives an illusion of comfort. Also, if you are too stuck in commitment, and it is too inconvenient too often, you will be unable to fulfill your commitment, and it will only generate frustration. Wisdom is to strike a balance between convenience and commitment because both bring comfort to the body, mind, and spirit."

Being committed at work was never an issue, but there was no doubt I needed commitment just to finish this course. Being with myself, observing my thought patterns and the corresponding restlessness in the body wasn't always comfortable. At the same time, I was intrigued by the perspective he was giving that seemed to lay the groundwork for realizing something much bigger in life. This Silent Meditation retreat was good for me and was exactly what I needed to unplug from the world and re-charge myself. I moved closer to the tiny television, so as not to miss a word of the knowledge.

"If you hold on to comfort, you can never grow. The more you let go of comfort, the more it comes along; in fact, it chases you. Holding on to commitment gives a direction to life. If you let go of your commitment, you cannot be

successful. Don't give up commitment for the sake of comfort. If you commit to something wrong, it is all right to let go. When you let go of some commitment, take up a bigger commitment."

Walking in silence to my cabin that evening, the sound of the leaves crunching underneath my feet seemed incredibly loud. I could feel myself letting go and settling down more and more. I decided to keep my commitment to myself, and with a sense of contentment, laid my head down to sleep.

To the wise, commitment is their comfort.

Commitment can only be felt when it oversteps convenience. That which gives you long-term happiness and short-term misery is best.

—Sri Sri Ravi Shankar

The next morning, although my body was in the present, my mind was right back to swinging between the past and the future. Although nothing outwardly had changed, I was back to being miserable with my own "mind-stuff."

Most of the people on this particular course were "old-timers" on the spiritual path, and they wanted to enjoy as many meditations as possible. That evening, I handed a letter to Philip, the course instructor, describing how this was the most boring thing I'd done on the path so far. I didn't understand what I was supposed to get out of it, I didn't like all the singing, and I was tired of sitting around and meditating so much. I wanted to leave.

Philip patiently read my long list of complaints before chuckling a bit. "It's just your own resistance. Be with the boredom. It's good." My temper immediately lit its fire. Boredom was good? The fact that I'd paid money and was unhappy with the experience was good? Noticing the cloud of doubt coming over my face, he went on to explain that boredom signified that we were evolving. He encouraged me to be with my own resistance; to just keep observing my own thought patterns and habits, without judgment of what is right or wrong. "Just relax and keep observing. The law of nature is that when we place our awareness within, what is negative dissolves and what is positive expands," he said with a genuine smile, adding an explanation for the Sanskrit songs we sang each evening.

"These songs are called *bhajans,* which are something like poetry in praise of nature, the Divine, God—whatever you choose to call the higher power who is running the show. It doesn't matter what you sing, just sing. Singing unites the heart and mind as one. It gives your left brain a bit of rest by waking up the right side of the brain!"

That evening during *satsang,* I relaxed. After just one song, my toe started naturally tapping to the rhythm of the music, and while I didn't know the Sanskrit words just yet, I had fun making up words—just to sing along. Walking back to my cabin, I noticed that I felt a lot lighter and more connected to everyone, including myself. As the chatter in my mind quieted down, to my surprise, a fresh perspective began to unfold around some of the challenges I was facing at the office.

The course ended the next day and while I was undeniably more at peace, I was ready for it to be over. After lunch, Philip asked us if we wanted to come out of silence or sit for one more meditation. I was the only person who raised my hand for the first option, while the woman next to me enthusiastically waved her hand for another meditation. Sneering at her, I imagined hitting her with the tambourine she banged at *satsang* every night before sitting up for one...more...meditation. Clearly, I was not enlightened yet.

Leaning against the cool glass of the patio door, I looked at Pikes Peak, the highest summit on the front range of the Rocky Mountains. No matter what nature threw at that majestic mountain, over hundreds of millions of years, it was still standing as strong as ever. I wondered what life would be like, to be that unshakeable no matter what nature threw at me; that's how unshakeable I wanted to become. Dropping my own resistance, I closed my eyes in acceptance of the present moment. And that's when it happened.

All the discomfort in my mind and body dissolved and I was in a state of *samadhi*—a blissful and deep state of meditation referred to as union with the Divine. For the first time since arriving, I didn't want to open my eyes when Gurudev's melodic voice began singing an ancient chant, indicating the meditation was over.

**Meditation can bring you to a
space that is unshakeable.**

Is it possible to perceive things clearly when you have stress in your nervous system? Meditation is the skill to calm your mind and get in touch with your inner source, which is joy and peace. It improves our observation of the world inside and out. It becomes easier to have a say over our feelings and emotions. Clearer observation means a clearer understanding of the situation, and clearer distinction of right from wrong, which inevitably affects our decision-making. Undoubtedly this will improve communication. When your perception and observation are clear, you know what to express and how to do it.

—Sri Sri Ravi Shankar

Determined to become free of my own "mind-stuff," and to be truly happy and free, I registered for the next course. If I was really lucky and stayed the course, I might just become as unshakeable as that mountain.

catapulted out of
the comfort zone

Over the course of the next year, everything in my life began changing. On one hand, I was the same hard-working traveling business executive during the week, who now meditated instead of meeting my colleagues for drinks after work. Instead of playing sports on the weekends and socializing, my free time was filling up more and more with the study of the ancient yogic sciences. I already knew what the world had to offer and no longer found it so charming. The Vedic wisdom had captured my sense of adventure, and it was leading me to places that very few people even knew about, much less had the opportunity to explore.

It is said that Vedic wisdom has been here from time immemorial and that no one person is responsible for it.

I'm told that thousands of years ago, *Rishis* (seers) gathered in a forest to meditate, and someone recorded what they learned. These philosophers and scientists were called 'seers,' because they 'saw' the knowledge. In such a deep meditative state, the *Rishis* were able to understand the subtle characteristics of the forces of nature.

I'd learned that it was rare to have the question, "Who am I and where did I come from?" More rare than this is to find a spiritual path and to be able to walk that path. And the rarest of all is to be in the company of the enlightened. It seems that more than 5,000 years ago and through deep meditation, the *Rishis* came to understand the origins and nature of the cosmos, along with medical science, mathematics, dance and music, statecraft and much more. Gurudev points out that the tradition of scientific inquiry found in the Vedas is still very much alive today and that our modern scientists are the modern-day *Rishis*. Like the sages of thousands of years ago, they're also exploring the universe. After passing on their knowledge orally for generations, it was finally written down in four main scriptures of the Vedas and its wisdom remains relevant even today. Learning about this ancient tradition and the power of the yogic sciences was absolutely fascinating, and I couldn't learn enough, fast enough.

The following year, plans started taking shape to host Gurudev over the Fourth of July weekend in Denver. The teachers did their best to recruit me as a volunteer, but I resisted. Just like any organization, I noticed that this group was no exception when it came to internal politics. My life was full and at that time, I didn't feel a pull to get more involved. I was traveling for business every week while enjoying the daily spiritual practice, weekly *satsangs*, and the occasional workshop.

After another Silent Meditation Retreat one weekend, my friends and I stopped for lunch. David had now become a close friend, and he'd been doing his best to get me more involved. The conversation floated back to the topic of organizing Gurudev's upcoming visit. For years, I'd organized many large corporate events in all kinds of capacities, and after listening to yet another conversation about what needed to be done, I waved a white flag of surrender. "You're a wonderful group of dedicated people, but you can't meditate an event into happening; it requires goals, strategy, and legwork." I handed David a napkin full of planning notes and everyone cheered. The next thing I knew, they'd appointed me as the co-chair of the event, which meant that I was about to meet Gurudev in person.

ancient **love**

Preparing an event for Gurudev meant securing a hall
large enough for a public event for about 1,000 people,
along with organizing a Silent Meditation Retreat for
another 500 people. We also needed low cost yet suitable
accommodations for the Guru and everyone attending
the retreat; no easy feat during the high tourist season
in Colorado. Along with the endless details that seemed
to grow by the day, I was tasked with getting media coverage for his visit, something I had no experience with.
Since our local chapter was still in a building phase, everyone was a volunteer. The national organization was also
fairly young, which meant our small team had to raise all
the funds in advance. We were counting on a lot. Denver
University finally came through as a venue for our Silent

Retreat, which meant everyone would sleep in a dorm room—including the Guru!

For some reason, I kept delaying registering for the retreat. After a month of wavering back and forth, David called to find out why I wasn't registering for the very course I was helping to organize. All I could tell him was that I was happy to be a volunteer, but I wasn't ready to commit to anything more.

Two weeks before Gurudev was due to arrive, I went for a hike and shared my dilemma with Marie, the woman who had brought me to my first Happiness workshop. "Let me get this right," she said. "This wise saint, who is responsible for giving you a technique that you say changed your life, is coming all the way from India to Colorado, and you're not sure you want to meet him?"

When she put it that way, I felt pretty silly. On the way home, I registered for the course, telling David to cash the check immediately—before I changed my mind again!

The excitement in the air was palpable as Gurudev's arrival day inched closer and closer.

Somehow despite all the chaos that comes with planning an event for a Guru, things were getting done. Our only concern was the public talk. The Fourth of July is known more for picnics and firework displays rather than spiritual retreats with a Guru, and our ticket sales reflected it. A call was made to India and Gurudev told us not to worry and that the venue would be filled to capacity.

The day he arrived, it was very hot, and in between fielding client calls and following up with reporters, I was also moving into my own dorm room and helping to set up a classroom for 500+ people. Wiping sweat off of my forehead, two senior teachers, Wally and Caroline, approached me, "How would you like to come with us to the airport, to receive Gurudev?" they asked.

The thought of meeting him at the airport was exciting, and I asked for a few minutes to freshen up before we left. "Sure, just change your clothes first," Wally replied. Looking down at my sporty designer walking shorts and polo shirt, I didn't see any issue with what I was wearing.

Both Caroline and Wally, who had been in the Transcendental Meditation movement, felt it wasn't appropriate to meet a Guru in shorts. I hadn't brought a change of clothes and Wally suggested I find something in Caroline's closet. The only problem was that I was a business executive and Caroline, who was from California, wore long flowing skirts was at least a size smaller than me. Wally pressed me to find something and in the end, the only article of clothing that worked was a pair of his white cotton drawstring pants. Wally is almost a foot taller than me, so I rolled up the legs of the pants and tied the waist as tight as possible. I'd never met a Guru before so I really had no idea if this was the best choice, but I followed their lead, trusting that they knew best.

The drive from the university to the airport gave me just enough time to become nervous. Sensing my anxiety,

Caroline smiled and handed me a long-stemmed red rose to present to Gurudev and coached me to just be myself. We had driven over in a big RV, so they both stayed curbside while I went in to meet him at the gate.

Standing alone with the flower shaking in my hands, my heart started beating very fast the moment Gurudev walked out of the jet-bridge. Dressed in flowing silk robes of white with a royal and powerful air about him, he walked toward me as I completely froze, uncertain of what to say or do. With a smile that exuded nothing but love, he took the rose from my hands as his ancient and wise eyes looked into mine for what felt like an eternity. The moment he meets someone he can see their past, present, and future, which he used to call "scanning." Even today, out of the hundreds of millions of people he's met, he says he's yet to meet anyone he didn't already know.

As we proceeded to walk toward the luggage claim area, out of politeness, I reached out to take the little black traveling bag from his hand. The black bag is the one personal item Gurudev travels with. Where the black bag goes, so goes the Guru. He gently resisted while I awkwardly insisted and he finally relented, and we walked onto the airport tram.

Wally and Caroline, who had been with Gurudev for a few years by now, were ecstatic to see him. Placing the *asana* (sacred cloth the Guru sits on) on the front seat for him, he took his place. Unsure of myself, I sat as far back in the RV as possible, while the three of them chatted in a friendly and easy-going manner.

However, I kept my eyes on the back of his head the whole time.

After a while, I felt something stirring in my heart and summoned the courage to share what was on my mind. "Gurudev?" I asked tentatively. "Haaa?" he replied while playing with his mala. Leaning forward I said, "Gurudev, I've been waiting my whole life for my best friend to come, and...and...I think it's you." Tossing his head back and laughing he said, "Ah...that's because we're part of a very old gang."

The next thing I knew, the RV had pulled up in front of the university, and the moment he stepped out, I lost sight of him as he was enveloped in the arms of several hundred devotees.

I was in a stupor. My head was tingling, and I felt a bit giddy. Gurudev went up to get settled in his room and Caroline turned to see what was happening to me. Like a nurse with a confused patient, she gently patted my arm and said, "It's *shaktipat*. Just go and lay down. It will pass." She explained to me that *shaktipat* is Divine energy transferred from a Guru to a disciple. I didn't really understand what it meant, but since I wasn't thinking straight, I went to my room to rest.

It was dusk by the time I woke a few hours later. I was the co-chair of the event and had no idea what was going on! I rushed to the main hall and was amazed to find everything had been taken care of, along with someone delivering my suitcase. I freshened up and changed my clothes but not before writing the first of many, many letters to Gurudev.

I never really saw myself as a religious person and what I was learning on this spiritual path resonated well with me. Still, I had struggled with some concepts and doubts about having a Guru. But after meeting Gurudev, I felt a strong sense of surrender. I shared what I was feeling in the letter.

Too shy to knock on Gurudev's door, I left my letter along with a box full of *I Love Lucy* videos outside of his door. I'd been a fan of the famous sitcom since I was five years old, and when I discovered that Gurudev was also a fan, I knew that he was my Guru!

Satsang was an especially big celebration that evening. Gurudev led a profoundly deep meditation, and afterward, I danced along with everyone else to the music. As we were leaving, David reassured me that I would be able to privately meet with Gurudev to ask him about my future plans. I was thinking of moving in another direction professionally and was considering starting my own company. But when the next day ended without a meeting, I started getting a little anxious. Later that day, David again reassured me that I would get to meet with Gurudev, but that it might not be private. That evening, in a small group I told Gurudev that I prayed to Jesus and many saints and now that I knew about Krishna and Buddha, I also prayed to them. It was becoming a lot of praying, but I wanted to be sure to cover my bases and asked him what to do. He laughed heartily and said, "Don't worry, we compare notes."

The next morning I was more eager than ever before to meet with him personally. A third time I was assured it would happen, but that there might be ten other people in the room with me. When the door finally opened, I was shocked to see the meeting room filled with people, wall to wall. Frustrated, I took a seat in the back of the room, doubting the possibility of asking him my question with any semblance of privacy.

Gurudev laughed and joked with all the devotees, gave blessing after blessing and answered all kinds of questions. Meanwhile, I wavered in my mind between getting up and leaving and waiting things out. As he interacted with the crowd, he kept tossing a red water balloon back and forth in his hands. For some reason, I kept my eye on that balloon, my anger rising higher and higher with every toss.

Finally, I decided to wait things out and the moment I did, I heard a loud "swoosh!" as the water balloon hit the brick wall just inches above my head, sending cool drops of water onto my hot head.

Stunned by what had just happened, I looked at the torn balloon and back at Gurudev. He was sitting as composed as ever, smiling right back at me. It was no coincidence he'd let go of the water balloon the moment I'd let go of my ego and decided to stay. As if on cue, the entire crowd got up to leave, creating a wide-open space for me to walk up to him and ask my question.

I told him what I did for a living and before I could mention my ideas for a change in career, he said, "You'll be a full-time teacher for the Art of Living Foundation." In spite of having no idea what that meant, I found myself saying yes and adding, "I'm a very good teacher," to which he promptly replied, "I know." How he knew this was as much of a mystery to me as my agreeing to do it.

Without a second thought, I asked him if I could leave my career right now. He instructed me to remain in my current career just a little longer and to watch how everything unfolded. He was scheduled to go to Colorado Springs the next day, and I took another day off, in order to follow him.

GPS didn't exist back then, and somehow David and I got lost driving up the mountain. By the time we arrived, all I saw was a wisp of white silk as Gurudev closed his door for the evening. Taking in the scene, there was no doubt that we'd missed something very special. The floor was strewn with rose petals and people were sitting around completely blissed out, intoxicated with love.

I traveled in the car with Gurudev the next day to the airport. David chatted with him about the events in Denver and mentioned all that I'd done in helping to organize things. Neither Gurudev nor I said a word, but when he informed Gurudev that I had no plans to take the next teacher training course, my face turned bright red. I had never even discussed the idea with him or anyone else and had no thoughts on the subject.

"Patti just bought a home and she has a lot of family obligations right now," said Gurudev, which was true. For the second time in twenty-four hours, I was dumbfounded that he knew something personal about me. "But you *will* take the next training, won't you?" he said, turning to face me directly, and I found myself nodding in agreement.

The next month Gurudev was back in the States, leading a series of knowledge talks in Santa Monica, California. I quickly rearranged my business schedule to attend at least one evening in his presence. He captivated the audience as he began to speak about Jesus as the embodiment of love. *"For centuries men have fought on this planet in the name of religion, in the name of God. They have no clue of Jesus. Of course this was already predicted by Jesus when he said many men will fight in my name."* There was pin-drop silence in the hall as he continued. *"Jesus, said 'I am your friend.' Krishna said the same to Arjuna in the Gita: 'Arjuna, you are my dear friend so I am giving you the highest knowledge.' This is the best way to bring out the teaching and to share the love. With the Lord you have respect, but with a friend you share your most intimate feelings, thoughts, ideas, and secrets. Where there is authority there cannot be love and where there is love, there is no authority. Jesus is opening his arms, saying, 'I am your friend. Don't put me on an altar. Keep me in your heart. Love everyone as much as I love you and as much as you love me. Share that with everyone else around.'"*

When he finished, it felt as though he had wrapped every person in the room with a blanket of unconditional love. Afterward, hundreds of people rushed to the stage for his *darshan* (blessings), and I followed suit. "Hi Gurudev, my name is Patti Montella. I met you in Denver," I said, unsure if he would remember me with all the people he meets on a daily basis. "I know!" he exclaimed while tapping my head with a red rose.

I flew home the next day, completely unaware of what was about to unfold in my life.

Gurudev is usually in the USA for Guru Purnima, a celebration that takes place every July during the fullest moon of the year. I was pretty happy when I learned that my birthday fell during a Silent Meditation Retreat he was teaching that month, at our Canadian Ashram.

The Ashram was fairly new at the time, which meant the facilities were rustic and sleeping accommodations were at a premium. My least favorite part of taking courses back then was having to share a room and bathroom with ten to twelve strangers. To save a little money and ensure a bit of privacy, my friends and I decided to rent a tent. It seemed like a good idea at the time, but since none of us were campers, the minute the heavy rains started, it was clear that we were all out of our element. It took only one evening of rough weather and trudging through mud in the middle of the night to use the bathroom for my friends to ditch me and the tent.

I elected to stay the course alone in the tent, while they slept dry and comfortably on the floor of the meditation hall, just steps from a bathroom. I'd camped once before while on a photographic safari in Africa and thought I had the grit it took to see the challenge through. However, the rain never let up, my clothes were always a bit wet, and the night I spotted a bear in the forest I resolved to never camp again—ever.

When I heard stories of Gurudev playfully spraying people with large water guns during *satsang*, an idea took root. His tradition is to honor people who are celebrating birthdays and anniversaries by calling them to the stage. In anticipation of the birthday celebration, I had hidden two small water guns in my pockets.

As soon as Gurudev finished the knowledge portion of the *satsang*, he called the celebrants to the stage, and I joined them, sitting right next to him. He smiled at me while placing a crown of flowers on my head as the crowd began singing the birthday song. I smiled back, while slowly pulling out the water guns and spraying him. His brown eyes became large with surprise as a small circle of water formed on his silks, right in the middle of his chest.

For a moment, I worried that perhaps I'd gone too far, when all of a sudden the tables turned, and he was dousing me with every bit of silly string available and spraying me with a giant-sized water gun. I unloaded the teeny bit of water I had left, while the crowd cheered on the fun.

The next day, during the afternoon meditation, Gurudev had someone read from the *Yoga Vasishtha*, an ancient spiritual text on the topic of liberation. A powerful sense of gratitude for being able to receive this knowledge washed over me. A few moments later, as they continued reading, I fell into a very deep state of meditation. Afterward, I felt Gurudev's presence before I saw him as he was leaving the hall, and struggled to stand up, out of respect. But I was still in meditation and unable to properly stand.

"Patti, sit down," he said, as I tried to stand a second time before almost falling. "Patti, sit down," he repeated, and this time I did as he instructed, effortlessly slipping right back into meditation.

Someone requested volunteers in the kitchen as people began to leave the hall, and I got up to join them. By the time I got there, the small kitchen was filled with people. When I went back up the hall, another meditation had started and the door was now locked. Unsure what to do next, I followed my intuition and walked over to Gurudev's *kutir* (the Hindi word for cottage). I had no idea what to do when I arrived, so I made use of the bench in the waiting area. After a while, two senior teachers walked by and asked me what I was waiting for. I innocently said that I wasn't sure, I just had felt pulled to come to Gurudev's *kutir*. They laughed, knocked on his door and were immediately allowed in. A few minutes later I was invited in as well and as soon as he saw me, he said, "Patti, I was thinking of you, and here you are!" It felt nice to know that I'd caught the wave of energy, on the subtle.

I took a seat, assuming I was in store for some quality time with Gurudev; however, the visit was over before it really began. Playfully, he inquired, "Should I have sweet or salty?" Seeing the confused look on my face he clarified, "for my snack before I rest...sweet or salty?" I recommended he enjoy both to which he smiled before scurrying up the stairs and closing the door.

obstacles on the
path of yoga

The spiritual path brings so much happiness and free-dom to the mind, yet at the same time, until you reach the final goal of liberation, many things can easily put a seeker off. The food on a course might not be to your liking, you can become upset with people, get stuck in conflicts, become ill, laziness can take over or you might struggle with doubts about the teacher, yourself, or the good in others. Gurudev points out, that until we are fully estab-lished in the self, becoming free of the cravings, aversions, and dualities in the mind takes commitment.

Yet the benefits of walking the path most certainly out-weigh any small inconveniences. Getting stuck in any of these things—these circles which are simply small and insignificant distractions on the way to enlightenment—is part of the Guru Mandala. The aim of a sincere seeker is to remain one-pointed toward the goal in order to come to the center, and the grace of a true Guru, a *Satguru*, is an extraordinary blessing in this regard. It's said that once you pass through all the circles of doubt, negativity, craving, aversion, charms, and ego, you become really strong. You become unshakeable.

Nine Obstacles On The Path Of Yoga
Illness, inability to comprehend, doubt, carelessness, laziness, lack of non-attachment toward the senses, hallucination, non-attainment of any state, or instability, these are the distractions of the mind which cause obstacles on the path.

—*Sri Sri Ravi Shankar*

I was in it all the way, settling for nothing less than unshakeable. My first circle to cross in the Guru Mandala came in the form of illness.

I was the healthiest kid in our family and always recovered very quickly. I've taken all kinds of risks both in travel and in sports, and up until now, I'd never broken a bone or needed a stitch. Yet, from the moment I stepped foot onto the spiritual path, karma came to me in the way of illness— lots of illness—and in a few cases, it was life-threatening.

The ancient wisdom tells us that as one moves on the path of yoga toward enlightenment, we encounter nine obstacles. Hearing this, I thought, *Well, at least, there are only nine—not ten!* By this time, I was moving toward becoming a vegetarian, as well as giving up alcohol in order to purify not only my body but my consciousness as well. As a result, I felt stronger physically, mentally, and spiritually than ever before, until a major health event unfolded that rocked my world.

I started having trouble swallowing and over time, my energy slipped away more and more every week. I went to the doctor several times, but all the tests came back negative; they didn't know what it was. After a few months, when my throat swelled up so much I had trouble breathing one morning, I drove myself to the emergency room. Unfortunately, the doctors at the hospital followed the same protocol as did my personal physician, and for a third time when I tested negative for strep throat, nothing more was done. When I left the hospital that day, I felt my life was ebbing away—quickly. Mustering whatever energy reserves I had left, I drove up to the mountains, for one last look. But when I reached the glacier, just forty-five minutes later, I didn't have enough energy to get out of the car, let alone walk. I drove back home, prayed for help and went to bed. Later that evening, I saw a red light blinking on my phone and was astonished that Gurudev had left a message for me that very morning. I don't know how I missed it and called him back immediately. "Haaaa?" he said, answering the phone. "Patti, you're not going anywhere. You will become a very old woman. Find a homeopathic doctor. There is nothing to worry about. *Jai Guru Dev!*"

I had never told him I was ill and I had never asked a question. So how, I wondered, did he know what was going on?! His voice, full of conviction for my own well-being, ignited my own faith. Unfamiliar with holistic medicine at the time, I had no idea how to find a homeopathic doctor, but I never doubted that with Gurudev's intention, a solution would effortlessly emerge. The next morning, I was able to meet with one of the leading ear-nose-throat doctors in the city, who had recently shifted to homeopathy.

"I believe you have a rare and serious staph infection in the floor of the mouth, called Ludwig's Angina, which can create enough swelling to block your airway. I don't expect homeopathy will work, but take these herbs for three days and let's see. If nothing improves after this, I'll connect you to a specialist in Denver who took over my practice. For now, place a note next to your bed, in case you have to call an ambulance that reads: 'Perform an emergency tracheotomy if I'm unable to breathe. I have Ludwig's Angina.'"

The homeopathic doctor had correctly diagnosed my condition and led me to the best ear nose and throat doctor in town. If the strong antibiotics I was given didn't work within a week, I would be admitted to the hospital. There was no way I wanted to enter a hospital with a staph infection; I could be in there for months, if I even survived the ordeal. For the time being, I took the medicine, stayed in the knowledge, and kept my faith strong while I waited out the week. Seven days later, I was showing signs of improvement and while the recovery was slow, it was steady. I eventually went back to work and seemed to be on firm footing, until I unexpectedly woke one morning with a high fever. Frightened, I called Gurudev. He gave me some specific directions and told me to fax him daily about my condition.

The moment I hung up from him, my body broke into a sweat and I felt strange all over. Alone in my room, I just stood there, unsure of what was happening. At the precise moment the sweating stopped and I felt all right again, I heard my neighbor calling my name. "Patti! Patti come here!" her voice had an unfamiliar sense of urgency in it. "Patti come here and see what's in your backyard." Slowly walking out my back door, I saw two pure white doves sitting on my fence. "I've never seen such a thing!" she said. "It's a miracle! It's a miracle!!" Smiling, I nodded my head in agreement.

It was clear to me that it was no coincidence that the white doves landed in my yard at the precise moment that my fever broke, literally minutes after speaking with Gurudev. When Gurudev called again, he advised me to find an Ayurvedic doctor to aid in my full recovery. I had no idea where to turn to find such a doctor and once again, within twenty-four hours of his direction, a solution presented itself. One of the leading Ayurvedic doctors in the USA at the time was staying with a friend only ten minutes away. He agreed to meet with me that afternoon.

This was my introduction to the healing science of Ayurveda. For several months, I took a range of Ayurvedic herbs and with each passing day, I became stronger. That fall I was well enough to attend my first phase of teacher training. Back then, there were just ten of us in the training, unlike the thousands who attend teacher training classes around the world today. The course was held at a monastery, which seemed an ideal environment for diving deep into the ancient Vedic wisdom with all the sanctity and reverence required.

Becoming a teacher on this spiritual path meant that I was now part of the lineage of enlightened seers who cognized the Vedas thousands of years ago. It was a humbling and thrilling point in life, as well as a huge responsibility. At the same time, it felt completely natural and there was no doubt in my mind that teaching this wisdom would become my life purpose.

the land of
saints and sages

A special international program with Gurudev was scheduled to take place in February 1998, at our sixty-five-acre Ashram in Bangalore, India. The program kicked off with advanced meditation workshops along with the celebration of *Shivaratri*, a powerful and auspicious day, according to the Vedic tradition. The trip included private air transportation with Gurudev and about 500 devotees to Ahmedabad, where Mahatma Gandhi's Ashram is located. From there, we would continue on to the holy city of Rishikesh, in the foothills of the Himalayan Mountains, for a meditation retreat.

After buying a house, my savings account was close to being tapped out, but I had no intention of missing out on an opportunity of a lifetime. I registered for the program and started making plans, even before moving on to the next hurdle, which was getting three weeks off of work. I was part of a new start-up that was about to launch the first online booking system for consumers during the same time that I wanted to be in India. I knew that this trip would be a significant milestone on my spiritual journey and prayed for help to clear any and all obstacles. I'd become friendly with one of our major accounts and during a sales meeting that my boss attended, she enthusiastically spilled the beans about my trip to India. No one was more surprised than I, when my boss acknowledged what an opportunity it would be to go to India and agreed to give me the time off. The day of the national product launch, a colleague sent me a message describing how baffled our boss was to learn that I was in India and that she had authorized the vacation. To add to the grace, when I returned to the States, I learned that a contract had closed while I was away, which I had barely done any work on. The commission from it not only covered what I'd taken out of savings for the trip, it covered all the unplanned extras as well.

Shivaratri is a Hindu festival celebrated in honor of the transformational aspect of the Divine. Shiva represents the meditative aspect of the universe, and it's said that meditation on that day is 1,000 times more powerful than any other day. It's an auspicious day for a spiritual seeker.

Gurudev describes *Shivaratri* in this way:

Ratri means 'night' and also 'to take refuge.' Shivratri is the night we take refuge in our spirit, i.e., Shiva. It is the time to celebrate the soul or consciousness within. During Shivratri, we take refuge in the Divine consciousness. There are two ways to do this: meditation and surrender. Surrender is having the faith that there is a Divine power that is taking care of us. Meditation and surrender bring peace and solace to us.

I was fully aware that traveling to India and staying at an Ashram would further catapult me out of my comfort zone in unimaginable ways, but I was ready for it and could barely contain my excitement.

My friend Victoria and I were traveling together and had arranged to stay with an Art of Living family in Singapore during our twelve-hour layover. Our hosts were kind and friendly people and we immediately felt at ease in their home. We quickly freshened up and sat to meditate before dinner, when something unusual happened.

Every time I closed my eyes, I felt like I was floating off of the bed. Was this levitation, I wondered? No matter what I did, the same sensation continued every time my eyes closed. Eventually, I settled into a deep meditation and when it was over, Victoria shared that she'd had the exact same experience. Neither of us had any logical explanation for what we'd experienced, and hunger quickly overcame our need to know.

Later on that evening, we asked our hosts if there was anything unusual about the room we had meditated in. They exchanged knowing looks and with great pride told us that Gurudev had stayed in that exact room during his visit to Singapore, just a few days earlier.

exotic **india**

In spite of traveling internationally since I was a teenager, India was different from anything I'd ever seen; it required thoughtful planning and a lot of flexibility. Travel time alone between America and India is anywhere between seventeen and twenty-five hours, crossing over a number of time zones. It's the second most populated country in the world, with more than a billion people, twenty-two major languages and hundreds of dialects. India is a diverse tapestry of colors, sights, sounds, smells and people of many different faiths, cultures, and backgrounds who co-exist, peacefully. I found it both pleasant and frustrating that no one seemed to be in a hurry, yet everything seemed loud and chaotic. The moment I stepped out of the airport, my senses were overwhelmed by the sheer volume of people. Taking it all in, I happily picked up my suitcases and got into our hired taxi.

We were told in advance that the Ashram could be rustic and physically challenging for first-time visitors from the West. So, instead of heading there directly, we spent a few hours resting, meditating and freshening up at a five-star hotel.

A few hours later, I woke up abruptly. "Victoria, wake up," I said. "I feel a pull!"

"Me too," she replied, rubbing the sleep out of her eyes. "We better get up and get to the Ashram right now. I think Gurudev may be looking for us."

We hurriedly threw our things together and headed for the Ashram.

In the late 1990s, Bangalore wasn't the high-tech city it is today. Once we left the hustle and bustle of the city, the ride along Kanakapura Road that took us through the countryside was peaceful and pleasant.

A few minutes outside the Ashram, our taxi driver told us how fortunate we were to have Sri Sri Ravi Shankar as our Guru. "Sri Sri is a Guru of the people. Most saints are not so available to their devotees. Sri Sri is a rare exception. You are most fortunate to be his disciples."

Victoria and I exchanged knowing glances as the 1950s car continued along the bumpy road toward our Ashram situated on the Panchagiri Hills. Before I knew it, we'd arrived, the door of the taxi opened, and I stepped foot into the next phase of my life.

The Ashram, which was once barren land, now held a number of structures built according to Vedic architecture, carefully placed amidst winding footpaths rich with foliage and flowers. The sweet fragrance of jasmine filled my senses as I skipped up the steps and into the round reception room.

"Hi, my name is Patti Montella; I'm from the United States!" I gushed cheerfully to the young Indian man with long black hair and big brown eyes, sitting behind the counter.

"Yes, I know who you are," he replied with a reserved and gentle demeanor, introducing himself as Raghu.

Bangalore Ashram.

I'd never met Raghu before and wondered how he knew me. Raghu, who went on to become Swami Sadyojathah, mentioned that Gurudev had been looking for us earlier that day. "When no one knew when you were arriving, Gurudev said it's all right. You would arrive by 5:00 p.m." Neither Victoria nor I had any arrival time in mind, yet when I looked at my watch, it was precisely 5:00 p.m.

A few minutes later, a tall, thin young boy with a wide smile named Harish arrived to take our luggage and show us to our room.

The paths in the original Ashram are rocky and some-what hilly, but in spite of it, this young man chatted enthusiastically while carrying more luggage than should be legally allowed for international travel!

We had brought all kinds of things to the Ashram, including too many clothes, packets of flower seeds for the Ashram grounds, school supplies and candy for the students, cushioned seats for meditation, our own sheets, dust masks, an endless amount of unnecessary items to prevent any kind of illness, along with Indian-style out-fits we'd paid way too much for in Denver. At a shop near the hotel, we'd also purchased buckets, scrubbing brushes and laundry detergent along with toilet paper—which we'd been told to stock up on. Doing our best to ensure our own personal comfort, we had to look completely ridiculous to the minimalistic Ashramites.

We all took a collective sigh of relief when we finally arrived at our bungalow; however, the code to unlock the door wouldn't work no matter how many times we tried it. A perplexed Harish eventually gave up, and we turned around and walked back to the reception desk to drop the luggage and set out to find Gurudev—which was actually my original intention. We found him out on a walk, making plans for a future lake and more buildings at the Ashram.

"Badda Bing, Badda Boom! Welcome Home!" he said, referring to the nickname he'd given me within a year or two of when we first met, and immediately inquired about my health. I'd sent him a message just before the trip to inform him that the ear pain had returned, which was the first symptom when I'd become so ill months earlier. If it persisted, I wrote, I would not be able to come to India. The very day he read my letter, the pain left as quickly as it had mysteriously arrived. "You're fine now, right?" he said, reassuringly.

I was more than fine now; I was supremely happy to be there and felt at home. We all walked back to the main grounds with Gurudev, and when it was time for him to leave us, I casually asked, "Gurudev, if you were a lock on the door of my bungalow, what would your number be?"

Without skipping a beat he said, "Try it one more time." Sure enough, using the exact same code all three of us had tried numerous times earlier without success, the door opened. There was no logic to it, and we just looked at one another in wonder before stepping into the quaint cottage.

The Ashram had recently built new *kutirs* (cottages) complete with bathtubs and little kitchens, which Gurudev had graciously placed me in, along with my Colorado friends. A few things still needed attention, such as curtains for the windows. Later that evening, as we were putting our things away, there was a knock at the door. When we opened it, to our complete astonishment, there was Gurudev, standing alone with curtains

India, 1998.

in his hands. "I heard you need some curtains. These were just made at our Ashram. I'm here to put them up."

There was no way four strong and determined women were going to let Gurudev hang curtains for us; he was meant for much bigger work in the world. He held his ground for a while, but when he saw we were not giving up, he handed over the beautifully sewn curtains. With a big smile he said, *"Jai Guru Dev"* (meaning Victory to the Big Mind) and waved goodbye as he continued to check on the rest of the international guests.

The Ashram was in its early years in 1998, and while we were building and expanding all the time, there were a few hiccups. It wasn't unusual to find electricity coming through the water while taking a shower or opening the toilet lid to see a cobra looking back at you! Every evening, Victoria waited outside while I removed all the large neon-colored bugs from our room. Ants were a regular nuisance, and since it's the one bug that bothers me, they seemed to know it and circled only my bed every day. Out of ignorance, I used bug spray on them, to no avail.

I was struck at how caring the local Ashramites were to the environment. Crossing the path to get up to the meditation hall one evening, I stepped on the grass. "Don't walk on the grass, it's sleeping," someone said. I don't know if grass sleeps, but her gentle approach toward nature touched my heart, and I never again stepped on the grass at night. I also didn't want to keep using chemicals on the ants, which wasn't working anyway, and one day someone suggested I just speak nicely to the ants and ask them to leave. With nothing to lose, I followed her suggestion and to my amazement, the ants left and never came back...but not before finishing our karma together.

That night during *satsang*, which was held outside each evening, a large flying ant kept buzzing around. We did our best to coax it toward the nearby bushes and once it finally left, I noticed a large welt forming on my shoulder. My friends had a good laugh calling it "ant-karma," while I rushed back to my room for an antihistamine to stop the itching.

We trekked up and down very rocky paths to and fro all day in the Ashram, from the meditation hall to the dining hall, to our rooms and to explore the grounds. Monkeys are everywhere in India, and our Ashram is no exception. They hid in trees, ransacked any rooms that were left unlocked during the day, and would even snatch the banana off your plate when you weren't looking!

Every day, sitting uncomfortably on a dirt floor covered by a thin rug, I tried eating food in the traditional Indian manner as my new friends did. The science behind this tradition is that when you eat with your fingers, you receive more *prana* (life energy) from the food. After a few days of dropping more food onto my lap than in my mouth, I finally got a fork.

It is part of India's culture to treat guests as God, and the Ashram went above and beyond to accommodate the Westerners. So much so, that I felt a pinch when arrangements had been made to provide us with homemade pillows along with toast and jam instead of the traditional hot *dosa* or *idli* for breakfast. While I've never gotten used to the Indian style of bedding, I'd be happy to enjoy a hot *dosa* and chai, any day of the week.

As a world traveler, I've always made it my habit to purchase and wear something representative of that country; whether it was a plaid wool cape in Scotland or a special perfume from Paris. Unsure of what time there would be to shop for clothes on this trip, I'd gone ahead and purchased a few traditional outfits ahead of time, but nothing compared to the beauty of the local fabrics and designs. So, I was delighted when friends took me shopping in the city. I think they had more fun wrapping me in yards and yards of beautiful silk from their country than I did. Once the *saree* was in place, they giggled while adorning me with all kinds of sparkling costume jewelry, along with placing a traditional bindi between my eyebrows. When I walked out of the dressing room, I felt about as comfortable as a giraffe in sneakers! It was going to take a little more time to adjust to wearing a luxurious silk *saree*, and instead, I settled on a simple outfit with pants.

Gurudev was incredibly busy with hundreds upon hundreds of devotees and distinguished guests arriving every day, so at first, I stayed away from his *kutir*. But, by day three, my longing to be with him was greater than my self-imposed protocol. I was helping to develop our prison program at the time, and clutching a business plan, I headed over to "*Shakti Kutir*," the tiny cottage where he lived, that doubled as his office.

Unsure of whether or not to knock on the door, I waited on the steps with a small group of people. A while later, a young man opened the door and called my name. For the second time in a few days, someone knew I was there, in spite of the fact I hadn't said a word to anyone.

I tentatively stepped foot into the tiny living room of the cottage and smiled from ear to ear the moment I saw Gurudev. He was sitting on a large and ornate wooden chair and smiled back. I walked toward him, in order to *pranam* (bow out of respect), but every time I moved forward, something kept pulling me back to the door. This went on a few more times, while fifteen pairs of eyes watched and waited. After yet another unsuccessful attempt to break free and step forward, I looked over my shoulder to see what the problem was. I was wearing a new outfit from India that day and had been struggling since the morning with the long scarf, which was now caught on the doorknob. The whole scene was like something out of an *I Love Lucy* episode, and with a red face, I untied myself while Gurudev patiently waited. Once I was free, I bowed respectfully as though nothing had happened, in spite of the giggles coming from the back of the room.

Shakti Kutir

The morning of *Shivaratri* I woke from a sound sleep at 4:00 a.m., with a strong intention to see Gurudev.

Rising as quietly as possible so as not to wake my roommates, I got ready, and once Victoria woke, I gestured for her to join me. The sun was still asleep, so guided by a tiny flashlight, we walked without speaking along the rocky footpath toward *Shakti Kutir*. Unsure of what to do once we got there, we just sat on a low brick wall, on the other side of the gate to his cottage, and waited. As the sun rose in all its glory, the birds began chirping, and the air was filled with the fragrant smell of jasmine.

After some time, when a young man passed us on his way up to *Shakti Kutir*, we asked if Gurudev was actually inside. He just smiled and suggested we keep waiting. A few minutes later, I heard what sounded like angels singing before I saw them. Coming up the path were at least twenty bare-chested Brahmin boys wearing the white mark of Shiva on their forehead, simple *dhotis* tied around their waist and chanting ancient Vedic hymns. The young boys who were studying the ancient wisdom had arrived to accompany Gurudev to the meditation hall for the sacred *Shivaratri* ceremonies.

Gurudev seemed to almost float as he walked along the cobblestone path toward the meditation hall. His head was covered with ivory silk trimmed in crimson, and he nodded ever so slightly in recognition as he passed. The boys followed behind on the narrow forest path toward the meditation hall, singing ancient chants to Shiva as incense circled all around.

Awestruck as I soaked it all in, I wondered if this was what it was like 2,000 years ago when Jesus walked the earth.

Gurudev began leading the sacred ceremony while I looked for my reserved seat. The meditation hall, which was filled wall to wall with people, presented me with a new lesson in customs at our Ashram in India. Doing my best not to step on anyone, and offering a lot of "thank you's and excuse me's," I proceeded toward my seat. But even the most docile elderly women refused to budge even an inch as I tried to avoid stepping on feet, legs and other limbs on my way up front. Everyone wanted to be as close to the Guru as possible.

I fell into my seat just as Gurudev began chanting. Effortlessly, I began slipping into meditation, a serene smile on my face, until the noise started—and it was loud. A group in the back of the hall had started beating drums along with blowing horns and conches, completely disrupting the peace.

Annoyed by what I took as an irreverent disruption, I craned my neck to see who was making the racket, but I could only see the bell of a trombone from where I was sitting. Gurudev continued the sacred ritual as peacefully as it had begun, and a few minutes later the noise from the back settled down. Once again, I settled into my seat and had just closed my eyes again, when the disruption began as abruptly as it had the first time. With no sign of an authority figure stepping up to put an end to the situation, I put my fingers in my ears and waited for it to be

over. My friends from India had to hold their sides from
laughing when I shared the story the next day. It turns out
the musicians weren't hecklers at all; they're actually part
of the sacred ceremony. The sound of the horns, bells, and
drums, I learned, signifies the awakening of consciousness.

Shivaratri.

We meditated on and off throughout the day and just
before *satsang* I sat with Gurudev and a small group for a
special Vedic fire ceremony. The ceremony is intended to
purify the environment and bless everyone with spiritual

upliftment, improved health and material gain. Afterward, we were invited to receive blessings from Gurudev. My eyes closed as I bowed in reverence and a sincere prayer spontaneously came to mind: "Please let me be an instrument for your work on this planet." As though he heard my very thought, Gurudev touched my head with a long-stemmed red rose just as I completed the prayer. When I opened my eyes to look at him, he smiled with that now familiar twinkle in his eyes.

It's said that on *Shivaratri*, the Divine energy that normally hovers about twelve inches above the earth, actually touches the ground. Since there is no way to know when it will touch the ground, spiritual aspirants stay up all day and night and fast throughout the day. After the fire ceremony, we enjoyed *satsang* with Gurudev, while everyone sang and danced in bliss.

A few days later, our merry group of about 500 seekers descended on the tiny Bangalore airport where two chartered airplanes were waiting to take us to Ahmedabad.

I quickly checked in and proceeded toward the gate where a huge crowd had already surrounded Gurudev. Several hundred people were all trying to squeeze through one small door with Gurudev that led to the waiting planes. Every now and then I could see the top of his head and a flash of white and did my best to follow—inching my way forward. Clutching a heavy suitcase, my body forced forward by the crowd, I was just a few feet from the door when Gurudev abruptly stopped in the doorway.

Everyone froze.

Every time he tried to walk forward, his *dhoti* was pulled so hard, it almost choked him. The crowd was so dense I wasn't able to see my own feet, but after the third attempt, everyone started stepping back to see who was stepping on Gurudev's *dhoti*. That's when I looked down and saw it...the beautiful piece of pure white cotton, under my shoe that led to the rest of Gurudev's *dhoti*.

My head snapped up and my eyes, full of fear, met his big brown eyes, full of love. He smiled at me as I slowly took a step back, releasing the *dhoti* and allowing Gurudev to proceed forward. Thankfully, no one was the wiser, and the next thing I knew I was right behind him and about to walk through the door to the waiting plane. Struggling with my heavy carry-on luggage, Gurudev reached out to take it from me.

"No, no, Gurudev, I cannot let you do that!"

"Patti, give me the suitcase."

"Please Gurudev, I can't. I just can't," I said, imagining a crowd of angry devotees hauling me off if they saw him carrying my luggage on top of the *dhoti* incident.

"Patti, it's too heavy for you. Give it to me."

I had to think quickly: "Can we make a deal? You carry one handle and I'll carry the other?" I couldn't bear the idea of my Guru carrying my luggage.

And that's how we continued forward—each of us holding a handle with a single piece of luggage between us. When we reached the waiting airplane, he looked down at our boarding passes, smiled, and gave me the luggage. I proceeded toward my plane and he to his.

The flight was filled with one big happy international Art of Living family. We took over the PA system to sing while someone played the flute; the entire flight was one big party. We were met at the airport by a huge group of devotees and all kinds of celebration including musicians and youth wearing traditional clothing representative of their state. Victoria and I could hardly believe our luck when we arrived at the hotel and were accommodated in a luxurious two-floor suite. We had no sooner opened our suitcases to unpack when a waiter delivered steaming hot cups of chai and cookies served on fine china. "I can't believe all the special treatment we've received since we arrived in India, can you?!" said Victoria.

The Guru's job is to know when and how much to push his students buttons until they become button-proof. While it was true that our experience had been a magical and mystical fairytale up until now, I knew it couldn't last forever. We were, after all, on a spiritual journey and "*tapas*," or penance, is part of the quest toward enlightenment. Enjoying the present moment, I did my best to drop any expectations about what may or may not come next. Sure enough, after Ahmedabad we continued on to Rishikesh with Gurudev, when all the material comforts came to a grinding halt.

tick tock, **it's time**

As I boarded the bus that would take us from Delhi to Rishikesh, I was greeted by Gurudev's mother who was sitting with a friend in the first row. Although she was a tiny woman physically, she had a big presence. *Amma* (Tamil for mother) welcomed me with a nod of her head and a smile full of love. I took my seat toward the back of the bus and settled in for the twelve-hour journey, which turned out to be more like "Mr. Toad's wild ride!" at Disneyland.

Everyone shouted with glee as the bus lurched and jerked forward and we made collective intentions for one another's safety as it wound itself through the winding roads of the Himalayan foothills. The hours passed with songs, jokes, and the start of friendships that would come to last a lifetime.

When my stomach started grumbling, I remembered the small tins of food on *Amma's* lap. As luck would have it, a few minutes later all kinds of treats were being passed around. There have been many times I've seen small amounts of food expand in unexplainable ways to accommodate everyone who wanted to eat, as soon as Gurudev put his attention on it. And just like that—food kept coming from those small tins until we couldn't eat another bite.

Around midnight, we finally arrived in Rishikesh, the land of Saints and Sages. In spite of being tired from the long journey, my energy shot up at the site of Gurudev personally greeting each and every bus of weary travelers. His level of awareness and dedication to being of service never ceases to amaze me, from caring for the planet and all of society, to being on hand to care for each and every devotee arriving at the Ashram or noticing which plant needs attention as he walks the vast Ashram property.

Once, when I was traveling with Gurudev, I'd taken out an in-flight magazine so that we could look at a map of the United States. We were discussing which cities in the country needed an Art of Living teacher, and I'd folded some pages back so that we could see the map easier. Afterward, as I placed the magazine back into the seatback pocket, Gurudev leaned forward, took it back out, folded it properly and returned it to its original position. "Patti, we are here to walk like a cloud on this planet. When we leave a place, there should be no sign that we were ever there." *That's* how lightly he walks on the planet.

Rishikesh is known as the yoga capital of the world. Saints and seekers have been meditating in this holy city on the banks of the sacred Ganges River since ancient times. Non-vegetarian food and alcohol are prohibited and the Ashrams all have curfews. It's considered a great blessing to be able to visit Rishikesh. At the time, it was very unusual to see even one Westerner, let alone hundreds, and we were all grateful to Gurudev for making the arrangements.

In spite of the late hour, the enthusiasm of the young men who arrived to load our luggage was as bright as the stars in the sky. They cheerfully loaded our heavy luggage onto a bullock cart and we proceeded to our room. The buildings were quite old and made of concrete, including the stairs, and the minute the door to our room opened, we knew that luxury time had officially come to an end!

Victoria, who keeps a pristine home decorated in mostly white, froze at the site of the dark and dingy room with a single lightbulb hanging over a dismal sink. Grabbing a small broom, I enthusiastically started sweeping while she replaced the sheets on the bed with our clean sheets from home. Grateful for the antibacterial soap I brought, I scrubbed the sink while she replaced the musty and scratchy blankets with our large woolen shawls. We started feeling better about the monastic accommodations until I opened the door to the bathroom and shower area. "Oh my God!" I shrieked. The shower and toilet were like nothing I'd ever seen or could have even imagined a bathroom to be. The toilet consisted of a porcelain seat lying flat on a concrete floor and the shower was no more than a spigot unceremoniously protruding from the concrete wall. I turned the water on and groaned; it was ice cold. Rishikesh is at the foothills of the mountains, which means mornings and evenings are very cold. To make a difficult situation worse, the only source of light in the toilet/shower area was a tiny window full of cobwebs.

With no choice other than to deal with our new surroundings, we lit a candle and placed a photo of Gurudev on the nightstand. Together, we counted off everything we were grateful for, which allowed our minds and bodies to settle down and go to sleep. The next morning, the sun was out, the birds were singing, and we were ready for the next adventure.

Rishikesh instantly became one of my favorite places in the world. Every day was filled with long meditations and knowledge sessions with Gurudev, along with rocking *satsangs* set against the beauty of the Himalayan Mountains. To this day, I still frequent the little shop where my friends and I would sit over chai and toast every morning before going to our courses. The narrow streets of the city are lined with tiny shops tightly squeezed next to one another overflowing with incense, jewelry, Rudraksha beads (holy beads), photos of saints, spiritual books, shawls, and a wide assortment of all kinds of trinkets, while the air is filled with the fragrance of incense, the sounds of tinkling bells indicating the start of yet another *puja*, and the sweet echoes of *bhajans* being sung in the distance. Saints, *sannyasis*, and travelers from all over the world huddle around steaming kettles of chai while enjoying a *dosa* or *idli* for breakfast. The exotic scene along the banks of the powerful Ganges River fills the senses, which makes for deep meditations on the beach, in a meditation cave or at an Ashram.

I had a question on my mind ever since meeting Gurudev, and one evening during *satsang* I finally mustered enough courage to ask it. "Do we find you as our Guru, or do you find us?" As though he was expecting the question to be asked, he smiled and took a moment or two to reply. "It can be either way." He then paused, and looking directly at me, added, "And sometimes you make a pact."

It's believed that taking a dip in the Ganges River, considered by Hindus as the holiest of rivers, removes all past sins, and Gurudev had thoughtfully arranged for us all to take this sacred step in his presence. When the day for our dip with him finally arrived, it was very exciting and we ran like children toward the river. Clueless as to what to do next, we waited for Gurudev to arrive. Stepping into the water, he had the men gather on one side of the river and directed the women to huddle on the other side—so that we could face one another. I was in the front row, along with several friends, looking directly at Gurudev and waiting for his signal that it was time to take a dip.

Gurudev smiled, then pinching his nose with a bit of mischief in his eyes, he very, very slowly submerged himself into the sacred river. It seemed like he was moving in slow motion so that we could observe every...single...freezing...cold...sensation...of the mountain water. Following his lead, once I was submerged in the icy river, I shot right back up like a rocket. Watching all of us shrieking and squealing from the freezing cold water, Gurudev threw his head back laughing, pinched his nose again and down we went, two more times.

Rishikesh.

Cold, wet and happy, the entire crowd wildly cheered as we rose from our final dip. Happily shivering and toweling off afterward, I wondered if the slowness of the dip was required, or if like Krishna, known for his playful manner thousands of years ago, our Guru was having a little fun?

Gurudev explained that taking a dip in holy water to be free of our sins is blind faith and that we can be rid of our sins just by remembering God. Still, I welcomed the ritual and felt happy, free, and grateful afterward, as though I'd been gifted a new start in life.

<hr />

I was constantly concerned about catching some kind of bacteria during my trip. Cows are deeply respected in India and wander freely up to the tea stalls, in the middle of the highways and all around the villages and cities. Where cows roam, so roams cow dung, which led to a self-imposed policy of carrying antibacterial wipes and wearing tennis shoes with socks at all times, in spite of the intense heat. Another policy I had was to never leave my room without a bottle of grapefruit extract to minimize any possibility of drinking water contaminated with bacteria, and a supply of medicines and other supplements. I was paranoid about staying clean and free of disease, which is why what happened next was so funny.

During the excitement of running to the Ganges with Gurudev, I had worn sandals, completely forgetting my

tennis-shoes-and-socks only policy. Rushing to catch up
with the crowd following Gurudev after our dip in the
river, I slipped into the thin, open-toed rubber shoes.

I'd only taken a few steps when I stopped in my tracks.
Looking down, I saw my worst fear on this trip manifested—my right foot was stuck in the middle of a large,
fresh, warm pile of cow dung. Screaming at the top of my
lungs, I ran back to the water to rid my foot of the unwel-
come gift of India, while a group of toothless Sadhus,
watching the scene unfold, held their sides from laughter.

In Rishikesh with Gurudev, 1998.

After cleaning up, I met up with some friends on our way to the meditation hall, when a slobbering cow approached me. In a firm tone, I told it to go away since I'd already had enough of cows for one day. Not wanting to disrespect the cow or any of the local people, I became a little concerned when it continued following me. My friends teased me that I now had "cow-karma" and suggested I speak to it kindly, a tactic that had gotten rid of the ants in my room. I finally relented and bought a loaf of bread at a little shop. Slice by slice, I fed the cow while giving it compliments, hoping that no one I knew saw me! This cow was either the biggest scam artist in Rishikesh or I'd finished another karma—either way, once the loaf was gone, it walked away. I hurried toward the meditation hall and caught up with Gurudev, who was out for a walk.

I'd had a familiar feeling ever since I'd arrived in Rishikesh and asked him about it.

"Gurudev, have I been here before with you?" I asked.

"What do you think?" he replied.

"Yes, I think so. I can't remember anything, but it feels like I was here before, and I made some kind of mistake."

"Like the movie *Groundhog Day*," he replied, laughing.

As would happen time and again over the years, his answer was so surprising I was speechless. Not only did he know my past, he also knew about a current Hollywood movie. "Groundhog Day" is a movie about a man who doesn't treat people kindly, and keeps waking up to the same day over and over again until he makes amends and gets it right.

One morning, after exploring the ancient meditation caves along the Ganges River, I came upon a Vedic priest performing a marriage ceremony for a couple from America. *Pitaji* and *Amma*, Gurudev's parents, were inconspicuously sitting on a bench and motioned for me to join them. For the next hour, they each took turns explaining every step of the auspicious fire ceremony to me. It was a precious experience and was also the last time I would see *Amma* before her passing the following year.

Just before I was scheduled to return to the USA, I felt a pull to see Gurudev and set off to find his *kutir*. There were no guards in those days to keep throngs of people away from Gurudev and I was able to simply walk up the old crooked and narrow staircase to his suite. I was surprised when the door opened and there was Gurudev, sitting with a few devotees in a room that was exactly like the one I was staying in, the only exception being the decorations. I didn't say a lot to him in those days; there didn't seem to be a need for many words. I *pranam*ed and to my surprise, these words fell from my mouth: "Is it time?"

"Yes," he replied.

"It's time?!" I asked again, a little anxiously.

With a big smile, he replied again, "Yes!"

"I'm the only breadwinner. There is no spouse, no family money, and very little savings," I said.

"I know," he replied.

"What will I do?"

He simply said, "Many things. I will tell you." To this day, I don't understand why I simply got up and left after such a life-changing moment, but I did. And, true to form, I didn't do it very gracefully.

Nothing can be fulfilling in life without doing some *seva* (service) for others.

There is a joy in giving and your nature is joy. Our first and foremost commitment is to do *seva* in the world. The very thought "I am here in this world to do *seva*," dissolves the "I," and when the "I" dissolves, worries dissolve. *Seva* is not something you do out of convenience, or for pleasure. The ultimate purpose of life is to be of service. When you make service the sole purpose of your life, it eliminates fear, brings focus in your mind, purposefulness to your action, long-term joy and maybe short-term problems!

—Sri Sri Ravi Shankar

I was so stunned by the news that I became a little disoriented. When I stood up to leave, I didn't know where the exit was and opened the door to his private room in error. Turning around, a little embarrassed, I laughed and said, "Whoops! That's not right!" Gurudev simply sat and watched, as though he was watching a comedy on TV. I finally found the right door and exited back down the old wooden stairs, just as my friend Dean was walking up the same narrow staircase. In a daze, I looked at him and said, "It's time."

"Time for what?" Dean asked. But I never answered. Instead, I went straight to my room to share the news with Victoria.

The next morning, my mind was racing with all kinds of questions: When, exactly, would my transition from corporate to spiritual life take place? How will my career come to an end? How will I earn money and where will I live? What's my next step?

And true to his role as my teacher, Gurudev stayed silent, leaving me to manage my own mind.

Dedicating my life to being of service to society was a calling. There's no right or wrong way to embark upon this spiritual path; it's different for each of us. At the ocean, some people walk along the beach, some pick up seashells, and others go deep-sea diving. Some people come to our workshops and learning the breathing and meditation practices is enough for them. Others are more inclined toward service projects, teaching, singing, or administration. For me, jumping in with both feet and taking every opportunity to be of service was the only way.

The last night in Rishikesh was interesting and entertaining. We went from a week of peace and celebration to chaos, as all the Westerners prepared to return home. I let go of any worries about my future for the time being, since organizing our luggage in time for our impending departure was more than enough to handle. What seemed like a simple enough task became a frenzy of disjointed activity with several hundred people trying to get situated all at once, and the chaos lasted very late into the night. The original idea was for everyone to place their checked luggage in a holding area the night before the buses were set to depart for Delhi. But nothing went according to plan.

By the evening, the normally peaceful Ashram grounds were filled with people shouting at one another, "Hurry up and finish packing!" while piling heavy luggage onto a bullock cart, as volunteers ran from room to room trying to help. After our luggage transfer, Victoria and I stood back, watching all the craziness taking place below. "This is a perfect example of organized chaos," I laughed, as we watched a very stressed transportation coordinator come unglued. When the situation still hadn't worked itself out by 3:00 a.m., Gurudev came down and brought order to the chaos.

The spiritual path is just that—a path. Everyone is moving at their own pace and doing their best to learn and apply the knowledge. The bus ride to Delhi the next morning certainly emphasized this point. I had loaded my carry-on luggage onto the bus early that morning, at the appropriated hour. Only a few others did the same, and after a while, with no driver in sight, I got up to see what the delay was. The transportation coordinator, who was even more frazzled by now, informed us that it would be at least another hour before we took off. Meanwhile, people were yelling at one another over carry-on space and arguing about arrangements in Delhi.

Someone had placed a navy blue blazer on an empty seat, and after even more time had passed, I moved it to another location and took that seat. I began reading a book by Gurudev, titled *God Loves Fun* and the timing of the passage I came across couldn't have been more appropriate: *"In nature, everything is just waiting for you to laugh, the whole of nature laughs with you. It echoes and resounds and that is really the worth of life. When things go all right everybody can laugh, but when everything falls apart, if even then you can laugh, that is evolution and growth."*

The bus slowly filled up with people and just when we were ready to leave, two hours late, the owner of the navy blue blazer boarded at the last minute. He told me to move out of his "reserved" seat. I just laughed and reassured him that we could switch later if it was really necessary. Huffing and puffing, he finally sat down and we got going.

People were de-stressing in all kinds of ways, and at one point the couple who had just gotten married were so upset that they started threatening each other with divorce! I chuckled, recalling Gurudev's point about shaking hands with disturbance in order to know peace, and consciously steadied myself. The more people became upset, the more it all seemed like a funny movie to me. I laughed and made wisecracks under my breath, much to the annoyance of the man in the navy blue blazer.

"You ought to be a stand-up comic," he said through clenched teeth, which only made me laugh more. By the time our bus pulled up in front of our hotel in Delhi, I was ready for some peace and quiet.

Grateful for clean, fresh linens and a hot shower, I enjoyed a nice long meditation followed by a nap. Everyone seemed to have done the same because by dinner that evening, the same people who had been screaming at one another earlier were now laughing and enjoying one another's company. India is truly a land of opposites. One day, I was in a meditation cave, and the next night, I was dancing under the light of a silver disco ball in a hotel. Anything and everything is possible on this path.

A deep transformation had unfolded within me while in India; I was not the same person when I returned home. Yet, I had to work and life quickly got back to being busy. I continued volunteering and teaching on the weekends wondering when the change from worldly life to spiritual life would happen.

Gurudev was scheduled to arrive in Jackson Hole, Wyoming, that summer. My back had been giving me trouble for a while and the night before my friends and I were set to drive to Wyoming, my muscles were so weak, I couldn't even stand. Determined to make the trip, I laid down in the back seat of the car for the entire nine-hour journey. The minute I entered the home where Gurudev was staying, all the muscle contractions and pain vanished, and I was able to stand up straight. "That's the power of being in the Guru's presence," said a friend, who'd experienced a spontaneous healing herself in Gurudev's presence.

After our meeting with Gurudev, we began preparing lunch for everyone. As soon as everyone was settled, I went upstairs to find Gurudev. Tentatively opening his door, I was relieved to see a few other teachers already sitting with him.

"How is Patti?" he asked, and I surprised myself when I blurted out, "Something has to go! Most of my office is now full of brochures about the course. I'm not giving 100 percent to the Art of Living and I'm not giving 100 percent to my job!" He just smiled at my outburst and said, "Patti will be the President of the International Association for Human Values."

Wyoming, 1998.

The who of the what? Gurudev explained that the organization would initially focus on providing homes, healthcare, education in hygiene and human values, and harmony in diversity. And, just as I did in India earlier that year, I nodded and left the room without another word. He was giving a public talk in town that evening and there was work to be done.

The next day, we took a trip to the Grand Tetons with Gurudev. He admired the majestic beauty, mentioning that this part of the country reminded him of Kashmir and of what the planet looked like before it was inhabited. Along the way, we stopped on a footbridge to admire the flowing river. I don't know what happened, but somehow while standing next to him I floated away, losing all sense of time and place while gazing at the water. The next thing I knew, everyone had left and I had to run to catch up.

The following morning, our small group gathered at the airport to see Gurudev off. I had something on my mind that I wanted to ask him but felt shy to bring it up. Sensing this, he took me aside to speak privately. I told him that I'd been waking up out of a sound sleep at exactly 4:10 a.m. for months now and didn't know why it was happening or how to stop it. Every time I awoke, it felt as though someone was in the house or outside of the house, and living alone, I was frightened. He told me to use a chant of protection I'd learned and touched my head with a long-stemmed red rose. I never woke frightened in the middle of the night again.

I was turning forty years old and my friends were planning a party for me that weekend. The night before the celebration, my boss called to say that she wanted me to fly out the next morning for a client meeting. Needless to say, the turn of events was disappointing, but I didn't handle it like I would have before embarking on this path. Instead, I took the change of plans in stride, my friends and I met for a quick dinner and I saw the situation as validation that I was making the right decision in leaving my career. When I returned later that evening, I received another surprise, which was much more pleasant than the call from my corporate boss. Gurudev called to wish me a Happy Birthday and had everyone in the room sing along; it made my night. More and more, the knowledge was coming alive.

Later that summer, when Gurudev returned to Denver, things were in motion to bring my career to a close. My director did his best to persuade me to stay with the company, but it was time to move on. The day I officially quit, I drove Gurudev to an event, as he shared his vision for the International Association for Human Values (IAHV) in greater detail. One day, I was a corporate executive and the next day, I was stepping into the unknown, as a globe-trotting yogi for one of the most renowned Gurus of the twenty-first century. It was thrilling!

Gurudev was set to give a talk to a sold-out crowd that evening and invited me to give a short introductory talk before he arrived. While the assignment was an honor, I was terrified; I'd never given a talk to such a big crowd and had only completed the first level of my teacher training. To make things even more interesting, he continued changing the topic I'd speak on all day long, making it impossible for me to prepare. Just as I was walking out the door to meet a reporter, he changed it one last time. I was very nervous about making a mistake and embarrassing myself—or worse yet, making the Guru or the foundation look bad. A friend encouraged me to live in the present moment, to have faith in myself, and to relax. Since I had no time to do anything else, I followed his advice and learned a valuable lesson.

Rushing out of the interview, I made it to the stage just in time. Standing in front of 500-plus people, I took a microphone in my hand for the first time as a public presenter. After taking a long slow deep breath, I welcomed the audience and began sharing the value of the breath in managing our mind and emotions. It took just two sentences to realize that I was in my element on stage. Because Gurudev had purposely not given me any time to prepare, I was a lot more natural and was even able to joke a little with the audience. The experience strengthened my self-confidence considerably. When I saw Gurudev afterward, he congratulated me and added, "I know you better than you know yourself."

As my last day at work approached, I found myself contemplating the idea of a romantic relationship and made plans to connect with someone I was interested in. The very next afternoon I got a message that Gurudev was trying to reach me. When we finally spoke that evening, he said that he had been thinking about me since the day before and that he wanted me to live at our German Ashram for several months.

"When should I come, Gurudev?"

"Right away. *Jai Guru Dev!*"

Deep down I intuitively knew that now wasn't the time for romantic distractions. I canceled the plans I'd just made in order to move toward something much greater in my life.

from jet set life
to ashram life

The Grace of the Master, of the Guru, is like a lit candle that can light another candle. Only one who has, can give. One who is free can free you. One who is love can kindle love. Most important is the Grace of the Guru and even that you can only get when you have some Divine Grace. Such company is difficult to get. Millions of people are there on this planet. Not everybody will get in touch with the one who has attained it. The Master, the Satguru, does not come in all ages, only once in a while. It is very difficult to get. You may walk by a Jesus, a Buddha, or Krishna and you may not notice him at all. The company of the Divine, the Guru or an Enlightened one is bestowed upon you unconditionally. It comes to you out of their Grace, because of their love for you.

—Sri Sri Ravi Shankar

The one and only blow-up I've ever had with my father was the day I told him I was leaving my career to dedicate my life to service for humanity as a spiritual teacher. Yoga and meditation practices were foreign concepts to most people in the West at the time, and while esteemed Gurus from India, including Paramahansa Yogananda and Maharishi Mahesh Yogi, had shared the Vedic wisdom in America, it had only been a few years since the controversial Rajneesh movement had captured the headlines for its hostile behavior and its Guru, Osho, had been deported.

Giving yourself to a cause that is greater than yourself is both a blessing and a sacrifice. I was embarking on a transformative journey where I was choosing to exchange material and worldly pursuits for spiritual life. Gurudev describes this as *sanyas*, which is living life with 100 percent dispassion and 100 percent bliss. It was a vision that seemed far from view, but I was willing to give it all I had.

I'd let go of a big salary and was now living on a small stipend, which was just enough to cover my basic needs. No longer able to afford an apartment, let alone a mortgage, I put my house on the market.

It took a number of conversations to help my family come to terms with my decision. I understood that my choice was unconventional, yet at the same time, I had to honor my truth. Through the years, my parents came to respect what I chose to dedicate my life to, and while I lost a few friends over my decision, those who were meant to stay in my life did.

Just two weeks after walking out of my former life, I was on a plane headed to Germany to live at our Ashram in the Black Forest. As the train wound its way from Frankfurt toward the tiny village of Oppenau, the magnitude of what I was doing hit me like a ton of bricks.

all kinds of
assorted nuts

I was becoming more accustomed to the fact that our foundation was a heterogeneous one-world family and that Gurudev welcomed everyone. But living this knowledge as a way of life meant that I was going to have to stretch my comfort zone in ways I could not imagine.

Our programs brought academics, leaders of industry, heads of state and even royalty to the path while also making room for some very unusual and interesting characters. Standing on the platform between two train cars, I breathed in the fresh air and laughed to myself, remembering an exchange between Gurudev and one such character.

Diane was a middle-aged woman from the heartland of America. The first time I met her was on a walk with

Gurudev in Lake Tahoe, California. Although she hadn't gone swimming, she had wrapped a large white towel around her head like a turban and was walking backward in front of Gurudev. She spoke complete nonsense while Gurudev continued walking forward patiently listening to her constant chatter. "Walking backward with a towel on my head while talking to Gurudev is one of my *siddhi*'s," Diane said, proud of herself. I had to stifle my laughter. A *siddhi* is a mystical power and I seriously doubted that this was the special ability the Divine had in mind for the enlightened.

One overseas flight and three trains later, I was the only passenger to disembark in the tiny station of Oppenau, Germany. Hauling my heavy luggage off the train, I looked around, but no one was there to meet me. Smiling at the kind station master, I left my bags and looked outside for any sign of an Art of Living representative, but the streets were empty. After twenty minutes or so, I became a little nervous. The station master didn't speak English and I didn't speak German. Cell phones weren't common at the time, and I had no change for the pay phone. I did my best to communicate with a taxi driver who drove up, but it turned out to be a lost cause. Once I was back inside, I started pointing to the address for our Ashram to see if I could get any reaction from the station master, but our signals, unlike the train, kept crossing.

I eventually gave up and wondered what to do next when a man appeared out of nowhere. To my surprise, he asked if I was Patti Montella, in perfect English. I almost hugged him, excitedly nodding my head yes. He said he had a message for me. "Your friends will be here in thirty minutes. They asked you to wait. They're on their way." I don't know where the man came from or where he went, but an hour later, two gentlemen hurriedly walked into the station—apologizing and telling me with great excitement that they'd just driven from Geneva where they'd been with Gurudev.

Werner, the older man with striking white hair, had a distinguished European presence. The younger man was quite tall with a very bright smile. "My name is Ewald. We're so happy you've arrived!" he said while enthusiastically shaking my hand. Leaving the station, Werner asked what seemed to me an odd question, "Do you like ice cream?"

"Yes, I like ice cream," I replied.

"Would you like to go for ice cream?"

Ice cream is one of my favorite sweets, but I found it a little strange that he wasn't offering me a hot meal after such a long journey. "Good!" said Werner, smiling brightly. "Gurudev said we should take Patti for ice cream when we picked you up." We stuffed my three large suitcases, along with ourselves into the tiny car and took off to a quaint, sweet shop in the tiny village. Three hot fudge sundaes later, Ewald, Werner, and I became the best of friends.

**To bring out the best in you, you must become
a true seeker, one who wants to know the truth.**

A true seeker will always put truth and service
before pleasure, along with a willingness to learn
with an open mind, patience, perseverance, and a
commitment with one-pointedness to the chosen path.

—Sri Sri Ravi Shankar

Moving out of life as an independent jet-set business-woman and into life as a modern-day monk in a matter of weeks was anything but easy. I was in Europe to help establish the IAHV, together with Werner and Ewald. Growing a new business was familiar territory; however, Ashram life was a whole new ball game.

I was averse to routines of any sort, which is why working for an airline suited me. Yet, running an Ashram requires everyone living there to abide by a regular schedule for meals, meditation, and *satsang*. My motto in life was work hard and play hard. So along with working, I started scouting places to go horseback riding and skiing. Both Ewald and Werner, who had lived at the Ashram for a while now, just laughed, knowing that there would be no time for such simple pleasures.

The accommodations at the Ashram were sparse, the schedule challenging, and the switch from living in my own home in a cosmopolitan city to a small room in an Ashram, with all kinds of interesting personalities, took some getting used to.

As a United Nations representative for IAHV, I regularly traveled to the UN Office in Switzerland. Every week, I'd catch a 5:00 a.m. train to Geneva and didn't return until midnight. At first the assignment was so inspiring

Germany, 1998.

that I didn't mind the intense schedule. However, over time, I became more and more disenchanted with the dynamics that come with such a complicated global system. One thing became abundantly clear during this time: if more leaders meditated, we could address society's most pressing issues with greater clarity of mind, creativity, and cohesion, and a whole lot more efficiently.

amsterdam

Our first IAHV event with Gurudev was set to take place in Amsterdam at the prestigious Intercontinental Amstel hotel. Ewald and I arrived in Holland a month prior to take care of all the details and to personally invite government officials, business leaders and ambassadors. We worked around the clock with a small local team to pull it all together, and it was a very exciting time. Every moment was special, from the day we received our first official navy and cream colored IAHV folders to our first RSVP from the office of an ambassador.

Like my colleagues, I wore many hats—from event manager, marketing specialist, copywriter and secretary to speaker and diplomat. The list of tasks required to pull off our first high profile event seemed endless and the process was fraught with challenges.

The first obstacle I faced was being asked to leave the home I was supposed to stay in on the very night I arrived. It turned out that my host had some personal issues and had changed her mind. With nowhere to stay and no budget for housing, Ewald and I drove back to a small town an hour away where we had just rented a space for a center. It didn't have any furniture yet, so I slept on the floor of the main room while Ewald curled up on a kitchen bench.

Wasting no time, we immediately went about arranging meetings and knocking on doors in an effort to fill the event with every influential leader who had an interest in supporting the mission of IAHV. Gurudev was not well known in Europe at the time, and we faced a lot of rejection in those early days including being chased out of a government building when we found ourselves on a secure floor.

The name of our organization—while impressive sounding—was a mouthful. And, more often than not, we didn't even get to finish saying who we were and what we were there for, before a secretary politely instructed us to leave our information and showed us the door. Nonetheless, we believed in our mission and were determined; so we came up with a new approach.

First, we started parking the beat-up old car we were using out of sight from the front of the buildings before we entered. Next, we honed our acting skills in order to get past the first gatekeeper and to keep going—using every bit of charm, confidence, and friendliness that we had between us.

Gurudev always says that our work is done through *sattva*—which is the element of purity, wholeness and grace. I was finding that the more I meditated and lived the knowledge, the more the grace unfolded in my life. Whenever I have opened a new city for our foundation, initiated a new project or led a team, I make sure to increase the *sattva* within myself and collectively, which helps things to move forward.

We remained vigilant in our commitment and the work required to see it through, and in no time, we had meetings with heads of industries, educational institutions and governments. By the time Gurudev was set to arrive in Amsterdam, we had almost 100 RSVPs for the event, as well as our funding.

The day of the event was a sunny and clear day, which reflected the joy in our hearts. Werner, Ewald, and I stayed busy at the hotel taking care of all the last-minute arrangements while another team left for the airport to receive Gurudev.

While I was excited and nervous, I also felt prepared, having rehearsed my presentation lines every day over the last week. Our guests were trickling in as we finished up a few last-minute details, when I heard a commotion. I looked up to see what was happening and was shocked to see Gurudev walking through the door. That's when I realized my first mistake of the evening—I'd never informed him of what time to arrive. His presence filled the room as it always does, with a royal and divine air of grace along with an undeniable sense of power and peace.

His arrival always takes my breath away, but this time, it did so for a different reason. Just twenty or so guests were milling about and I hadn't even finished placing the IAHV packets on all the chairs. To this day, I have no idea how it happened, but in the moments it took me to stop what I was doing and walk to the front of the room to start the event, all the chairs were filled. Nervously, I took the microphone, and as I began to welcome our guests, my heart almost stopped.

Gurudev was sitting in the front row just a few feet away, looking straight at me, his arms folded and a mischievous smile on his face. I'd been a trainer for almost twenty years and was comfortable speaking in front of a crowd, but this was different.

I was in a foreign country addressing CEOs and ambassadors, as well as my peers and my spiritual master. This meant that along with everyone else, Gurudev would observe every word I uttered, how I presented myself, and he would be able to read my thoughts. My palms started sweating.

Refusing to meet his eyes in order to just get through it, my voice shook as I began speaking. Before the next presenter came to the stage, I had to introduce a short video interview that Gurudev was featured in, along with the Dalai Lama and Deepak Chopra, entitled, *The Three Wise Men*. When it was finished, I invited Werner to the stage.

However, instead of introducing Gurudev, which Werner was supposed to do, he took the mic and said, "I think Patti Montella did a wonderful job and she should come back up and continue the program, don't you all agree?" He obviously was even more nervous than I was to speak in front of Gurudev and started clapping enthusiastically while beckoning me to the stage. The entire audience joined in and I had no choice but to unglue myself from my seat while screaming inside of my mind, "*What is he thinking?!*" I was not at all prepared to introduce Gurudev to the distinguished audience, especially with him sitting right there in the front row. I wanted the earth to open up and swallow me whole right there and then.

Taking the microphone, I willed my memory to recall the snippets of the introduction I'd heard Werner practicing over the last week while suppressing thoughts of clubbing him over the head with the microphone. To a devotee, there is none better than her Guru. I am blessed to be such a devotee. Knowing this may help to explain what happened next.

I took a breath in and looked directly at Gurudev, who exuded such a wave of unconditional love and support that I was able to continue. Still, it felt awkward referring to the video with him sitting right in front of me. Unsure of what to do, I remarked that while all the people in the video were very wise, we consider Sri Sri Ravi Shankar the wisest of all. Adding to my unprofessional introduction, I invited Gurudev to the stage by saying, "Let's welcome the man himself—Sri Sri Ravi Shankar!" The audience clapped enthusiastically and I sat down, completely unaware of my mistakes.

There was pin-drop silence in the room. Everyone was waiting with anticipation to hear Gurudev speak. "When we love someone very much," he said, looking at me, "sometimes we go a little overboard in our introductions." In a flash, I realized that not only had I unintentionally disrespected the other spiritual leaders in the film, our event sponsor was a close devotee of the Dalai Lama.

The rest of the event was a blur. After everyone left, I stayed back. I couldn't bear facing my peers, let alone Gurudev. Ewald tried to comfort me, but I was inconsolable. My lack of awareness had insulted two beloved spiritual leaders and had placed my own Guru in an awkward position.

After some time, I knew I had to face the music and we drove to the hotel where Gurudev was staying. When I walked into the room, Gurudev turned to the group of devotees gathered and said, "Patti did a wonderful job! Didn't she do a wonderful job?" He started clapping and everyone followed his lead while I stood there completely dumbfounded.

Rather than admonish me, he supported me through what had clearly been a difficult evening of firsts. I realized the mistake I'd made. All it took was a pinch of awareness and the loving support of my Guru to galvanize my resolve to do better next time.

The event turned out to be a success and IAHV continues to grow and expand in partnership with governments, businesses, and humanitarian organizations worldwide.

The deeper you dive into the self, the more love blossoms.

Everything is already there. All the petals are there, it is only a matter of time. When you know this, great peace dawns within you. Whenever you feel, 'Oh, I can't do it,' then you can't do it at all. But when you say, 'I can get over this, I can do it,' then that energy, the courage, enthusiasm, zeal, and everything comes. The path of spirituality inspires, it has always said, 'You are great, you are part of the Divinity, you are love, you are beauty, you are truth! To grow in unconditional love and in beauty, is spirituality.'

—Sri Sri Ravi Shankar

you lost your seat
for a bag of chips

Traveling with Gurudev is a little like riding a roller-coaster; it offers a complete range of emotions. The ride always begins with the initial thrill, then moves onto trepidation over unforeseen twists and turns, and at some point there may be a moment of fear while it goes up and down and you have no idea where you'll land. Yet, no matter what takes place, when the ride ends, you're left wanting more.

Keeping up with his schedule is not for the faint of heart. He sleeps just a few hours a night, rising before dawn to meditate and attend to millions of people, problems and global issues all day long—every day. And yet, he does it with an unending smile, as though managing all his responsibilities is as easy as picking up a feather.

He travels from continent to continent as often as we move from room to room in our own home. Gurudev is constantly surrounded by thousands of people from every walk of life, yearning for even a glimpse of him, which can become quite intense. Just walking from his office to the meditation hall in India, where thousands visit daily, people have pulled at and ripped his clothes as well as his hair. Out of devotion, he is presented with more food than he could ever eat—along with all sorts of interesting people and situations.

The first time I traveled with him by car for any length of time was during our return trip from Holland back to the German Ashram. There were just a few of us with him, and after a while, we pulled into a gas station to fill up and to use the facilities. I was waiting alone in the car with Gurudev, when all of a sudden I got the urge for potato chips, which was odd since I prefer sweet to salty. I did my best to push it out of my mind, but eventually I gave in. Reassuring Gurudev that I would be right back, I left him alone, without even asking him if he would like something.

As I pushed open the door to the store, an uncomfortable feeling washed over me. I stopped and looked back at Gurudev, who was still alone and just watching me, so I shrugged the feeling off and entered the store. When I returned with literally one bag of chips in my hands, someone else had taken my seat in the car. I had no choice but to jump in the back seat of a cold and uncomfortable van for the rest of the trip.

Four Benefits Of Having A Guru:
Knowledge, Movement, Achievement, Liberation
Sometimes we feel stuck in life. Events, situations, concepts can all make one feel stuck. The Guru's presence makes you realize that you are stuck and helps you to move.

Moving from where we are stuck to having the flow in life toward its ultimate goal is the second benefit.

To get what you want, you need guidance. You need someone to give you what you want. But then there is no end to desires and sometimes you are not even sure of your own desire. That is where the Guru comes into play. The Guru principle or Guru-tattva *will give you that which is good for you and not everything that you want.*

The fourth benefit is liberation or inner freedom. Guru does not let you remain in an illusory world but helps you wake up and look at what is the ultimate reality of the universe. That is freedom or liberation.
—Sri Sri Ravi Shankar

Gurudev enjoys surprising people and had called a devotee to tell them that we would be at their home in an hour for an impromptu *satsang*. I could only imagine the chaos that ensued after such a call! It was winter in Germany and when we arrived, the warm and charming home was a welcome contrast to the cold harsh weather outside. I hung up my coat and eyed a table in the front of the living room, decorated with a lace antique table-cloth. It was piled high with sweets, snacks and hot tea, all on fine china. At the other end of the room, a simple yet beautiful seat was prepared for Gurudev in the tiny living area. How, I wondered, had our hosts possibly prepared the room and filled it with so many devotees in less than one hour?

While everyone was arriving and getting settled, someone began singing a devotional song to Gurudev. I was sitting in front of Gurudev and looked up at him, my face beaming with love without a thought in my mind. The atmosphere was serene and peaceful...for a brief moment. "You lost your seat for a bag of chips," Gurudev said looking right at me. My entire body froze. He repeated the sentence, slowly, emphasizing every single point..."*You... lost...your seat...for a bag of chips.*"

Before I could even think of a response, the room filled with people and I had nowhere to go but to remain in front of Gurudev, burning with regret and shame over my stupidity.

I made a plan to rush out of the house and back into his car the moment the last note of the last song finished. Racing to grab my coat, I bypassed all the delicious snacks on the table our guests had provided. Without even a thank you, I threw all manners out the window in order to get to the car before anyone else did. It was unlocked and I sat down in the dark and waited for Gurudev before anyone knew I'd left.

A few minutes later, a young woman approached the car and asked me to get up so that she could get her hat. Resolutely I told her there was no way I was moving—how did I know if it was a trick just so she could sit in the

Guru's car? I wasn't taking any chances of being a fool for a second time today. She persisted until I lifted my bottom just enough so that she could grab the hat. A few minutes later, the passenger car door opened. Gurudev entered the car, and we drove home to the Ashram.

The next evening, our chef made a wonderful multi-tiered birthday cake for everyone to enjoy after *satsang*. Just as the cake was being wheeled out of the kitchen, the man who was supposed to unlock the door to Gurudev's suite before he arrived caught sight of it. He wavered between doing his job right away or grabbing a piece of cake. When I saw that he was about to make the same mistake I'd made the day before, I offered to bring him a piece of cake. Still, he hesitated. "Don't wait," I said. "Go directly to Gurudev's room. Do your job. I'll bring you the cake!" He finally relented and went up the stairs.

By the time I got up to Gurudev's room with the cake, four more people had arrived with huge slices for my friend. When the fifth piece of cake arrived, Gurudev said to him, "See? When you put the Divine first, all abundance flows directly to you." It was a lesson I would never forget.

the ultimate **relationship**

"I don't want to be a monk!" I declared to Gurudev, defiantly. I was fed up with living in a tiny bedroom, in a cold and dark building in the middle of nowhere and with some of the oddest personalities I'd ever encountered. The huge shift in my life in such a short time had gotten the best of me.

"Just be grateful that you came when we have a few things now," Gurudev replied while reading his emails.

"I need to have more fun," I added.

"Fun is limited," he said as he put the emails to the side. "Do you want a relationship?" he then asked, as though it was a very small desire.

The truth was that the only relationship I wanted was union with the Divine in order to be of greater service to others. He asked me a second time, and when I confirmed the same answer, he rose from his chair, looked out the window for a moment before turning to face me, "Then you focus on your Guru and your work and that's it." The power behind his words stilled my mind. He was taking responsibility to guide me all the way to the most cherished desire in my heart—an unshakeable state of inner freedom—which meant I couldn't fail.

One evening, Ewald, another friend, and I stayed up late into the night, partaking in what I used to jokingly refer to as, "spiritual gossip." What it actually meant was that we were gossiping about people we knew on the spiritual path while sharing Guru stories and some tidbits of knowledge. My friends were doing their best to answer all my questions about Lord Krishna and some of the Vedic traditions, which were still new to me, and in between we were wondering why various odd and difficult personalities lived at the Ashram.

I'd been fighting off illness since returning from Amsterdam and didn't feel well the next morning from having stayed up so late. The next morning, Gurudev called all three of us to his meeting room. First, Ewald was called in and left with his head low, then the next person was called in and left in the same way. When it was my turn to meet with Gurudev, I entered with trepidation. As soon as I walked through the door, he took one look at me and said, "How do you feel?"

Before I could answer, he continued in a firm, no-nonsense tone.

"Look at you...you have no light." I sat down, without saying a word. He continued, "What time did you go to bed? I'll tell you what time you went to bed—3:00 a.m.! What were you doing?"

"We were talking about Krishna and Vedic traditions. I have a lot of questions."

"You do not know who you are or what your capacity is. I'll tell you what you were doing—you were gossiping about other people and questioning why they are on the path. This is none of your business."

How in the world, I wondered, did he know that we had been speaking about people at the Ashram?

I hadn't paid attention to my health and had stayed up way too late over the last several months. At the same time, I knew that learning to control the senses, instead of allowing the senses to control me, is one of the six wealths on the path of yoga. Gurudev cautioned me not to stay up so late again, not to gossip, and not to miss one meditation just before handing me a bedtime of 10:00 p.m. I couldn't believe what just happened; I was a grown adult. But the next day, I was even sicker and had to leave the afternoon meditation. Just in case Gurudev came looking for me, I let Werner know that I wasn't well and had gone to bed. Sure enough, the moment the meditation was over, Gurudev went looking for me in the office. I endured a lot of teasing about being given a bedtime, but the truth was, the Guru is always taking care. I was so tired that as soon as my head hit the pillow I was fast asleep and happy for it.

the wealth of **faith**

Five months had passed and I was eager to return to the States. Gurudev was back at the Ashram and one afternoon after meditation, he asked who in the room spoke Spanish. I had studied Spanish and was almost fluent at one point, but I hadn't used the language in many years. There was no way I was going to take a chance of ending up in Spain for months by raising my hand so I sat quietly. In spite of Gurudev suggesting that I live as though the sky is my roof and the earth is my living room (as he did), I longed for the comfort of my own bed back home. Since I was the only American in the room, I was sure someone from Europe would be fluent in Spanish, but when no one raised their hand when he asked a second time, I had no choice but to raise mine.

"Very good!" he said, "Tomorrow, you go to Spain."

"*What?!!!*" I screamed inside of my head as my body tightened up with resistance. I did my best to play it cool and simply asked what I would do in Spain. "You'll meet the President of Spain and tell him about IAHV," Gurudev replied, as though it were as simple as going around the corner to buy a carton of milk.

The whole situation felt like a setup, so as soon as the session was over, I ran into the office to confer with my friends on how to handle it. Someone suggested I arrange meetings in Geneva with as many companies as I could about supporting IAHV projects in India, which was the one task I hadn't completed. Without professional materials to present to a corporation, I'd dragged my feet on setting up any meetings. Spurred on by the thought of my return to the States being delayed indefinitely, I scheduled five business meetings with top executives of multi-national companies within an hour; a task that could have taken at least six months in my former career.

Taking a deep breath in, I summoned my courage and knocked on Gurudev's door to give him the update.

"Gurudev I *could* go to Spain, *but*, I have five meetings set up in Geneva for Monday, including a meeting with the head of Nestle's Global Humanitarian programs.

"Okay, then you should go to Geneva," he said without looking up from what he was reading. Closing his door, I danced all the way back to my office, grinning from ear to ear.

The meeting with Nestle went well, and a few weeks later when we met a second time, I brought a teacher from India with me. I'd never visited a village in India and knew that she could describe the plight of the working poor in her country better than I could. The woman we met with was impressed with our work and agreed to fund a borewell project that would provide safe water for many people. As soon as we returned, I met with Gurudev to share the good news.

"You see, Patti? Whenever you walk with the Guru you always have everything you need. There is no reason to ever wait to do our work."

The time to leave Germany finally arrived, and images of hiking in the pristine Rocky Mountains began floating through my mind, along with the faces of family and friends.

One evening, I casually mentioned to a friend that I understood how Gurudev might prefer that I live at an Ashram, but I was looking forward to returning to my own home. The next thing I knew, Gurudev called me in to discuss my program in the USA. "Patti, you can live in Washington, DC, Los Angeles, or Chicago when you return to the USA. Where do you want to live?"

I enjoyed living in the west, but for some odd reason, I replied, "I'm an East Coast girl, so I'll go to DC" And then I continued, "Uh, no, wait a moment—can I think about it and tell you tomorrow?" He smiled and said it was fine. Carefully weighing the pros and cons of every city, the next morning I informed Gurudev that I'd chosen Los Angeles. "But you said you were an East Coast girl," was his response. My own words were coming right back to bite me. "I know, Gurudev, but I haven't lived on the East Coast for a very long time. I think the west is better."

"Is Chicago too cold?" he asked.

"Yes, Gurudev, it most certainly is. I grew up in Buffalo, New York. That was enough cold for several lifetimes."

"Ok, then you will go to Washington, DC. Sell your house. You can live with Neelam and Vinod. You'll be very independent with your own room. I will call them. You can live here for six months, and in the USA for six months. Pick out any room you want at the Ashram. Hurry now, it's time for *satsang. Jai Guru Dev.*"

I walked out of his room in a daze. In less than a minute, I was no longer living in Denver, I had to sell my home and move in with strangers in a city I didn't want to live in. Panic set in as my mind swung between gratitude for the work I was doing, to wondering if I'd made the biggest mistake of my life.

The next day I surveyed the Ashram and chose an ideal room with a private bathroom. It offered a lot more space and privacy than the small room I'd been living in. When I approached the Ashram Manager about my choice, he just laughed. "He is playing a game with you. There is no way you will get this room. By the time it's all done, you'll be living in the tiniest room available and sharing it with a stranger." My fire rose at his insolence, and I stormed off to look for Gurudev to be sure I had understood his direction. He assured me that I had, and that it would all work out.

I knew that if I didn't nail things down about the room now, it would be a problem when I returned. But the manager just kept putting me off, so I approached Gurudev about it again and he agreed to meet with us. Positive that the manager was going to be admonished for giving me a hard time, I felt confident about the outcome. I was in no way prepared for what happened next.

"Who do you think you are, requesting the best room in the Ashram when you are just starting out?" said Gurudev. I literally looked behind me to see if he was referring to someone else. The discussion continued for quite a while, with various room scenarios presented, including moving out every time my room was needed for a course participant, which could happen weekly! By the time the meeting finished, I was back to living in the same small room I already had. At first I was confused, and then I was furious; the whole scene felt like a betrayal.

"Patti, you will have your own bathroom. Even the most senior teacher here doesn't have her own bathroom. So, is everyone happy now?" asked Gurudev.

"Happy? I don't know what your version of happy is, but this face is *not* happy," I replied, before storming out of the meeting. After crying for hours alone in my room, I began packing up my belongings. I planned to ask my parents if I could move in with them until I figured out a game plan, which meant I'd have to listen to *a lot* of "I told you so's" at the very least. I'd walked out of a successful career and given up a luxurious lifestyle to do humanitarian work and it was about to be over in just a few months. The word "embarrassing" didn't begin to cover it.

Life cannot progress if there is no faith.

Shaking of faith and devotion sends you a message about the strength of your faith. What is the need to be afraid of? Shake it as vigorously as you can. I would say only that faith is authentic which stays even after shaking. This is a job of the Master—to shake the faith and let it grow stronger. The Guru doesn't build your faith but he shakes your faith. This is the strategy from ancient times. When the faith shakes, it reveals that it can be made stronger. If it is authentic, anyway it will grow strong. In the whole process, you realize this is all a mere play of mind. Faith and devotion were always present. Devotion towards truth can never disappear. This is maya (illusion) of the mind which makes you feel it is shaken.

—Sri Sri Ravi Shankar

I was angry and didn't want to chant another word of Sanskrit, let alone pray to anyone or anything for guidance. As the sun set, the room became as dark as my mood. *Satsang* was starting soon and I knew that if I didn't attend, Gurudev would send someone looking for me. With a frown set firmly in place, I sat in a corner of the large meditation hall, as far away from him as possible with the intention of withholding the one and only request Gurudev has of his teachers—a smile.

He entered the room, clapping small hand cymbals and singing as he took his seat. Scanning the room he found me, seething in the back corner, and gestured that I should smile, but I was firm in my resolve to remain miserable and alone in the corner. Normally singing in *satsang* continues for some time before Gurudev shares knowledge; however, after just a few moments, he put the cymbals down, and looking right at me, with a firm tone he said, "We'll start with knowledge tonight."

He began speaking about six wealths on the path of yoga, which are: *Kshama, Dama, Uparati, Titiksha, Shraddha,* and *Samadhana.*

"*Kshama* refers to tranquility of the mind," Gurudev explained. "When the mind wants to do too many things, it gets completely scattered. With *kshama*, you can focus your mind and be more alert. *Dama* is having a say over your senses; it's essential, because many times you don't want to do something, yet you still do it. With *dama*, your senses don't drag you; instead, you will say 'yes' or 'no' to the senses."

He continued. "The third wealth, *titiksha*, is endurance or forbearance. When difficult things come, forbearance allows you to go on without getting completely shaken and shattered. Opposites such as health-sickness, losses-gains...come and go; armed with *titiksha*, however, you aren't deterred by whatever happens. Often, whatever is unpleasant can become pleasant later on. These are the changes that go on in life. The ability to not get carried away by the events, the judgments, is *titiksha*."

My friends, who were sitting in front of Gurudev looked back at me, as if to say, "Are you listening?"

"The fourth wealth, *uparati*, means rejoicing in your own nature. How? By not doing things because someone else says or does something; by not laboring hard to win approval, or striving to keep up with the Joneses. Being in the present moment, being in the joy that you are, and discovering the ability to rejoice in anything that you do, that is *uparati*."

He pointed out that faith or *shraddha* is the fifth wealth. "Faith is needed when you have found the limit of your knowing. Your willingness to know the unknown is *shraddha*. It would be fanaticism to think there is nothing beyond. Absence of faith is doubt—in yourself, others, or the whole. Ninety-nine percent of people doubt the whole, because they do not believe that there is a whole that is functioning."

He added that the stairs to heaven are slippery and soapy, emphasizing the need to hold onto the railing of knowledge to make it all the way before leading everyone in a *bhajan*.

I felt my icy demeanor beginning to melt a bit, but I stubbornly resisted for a while longer. Gurudev stopped the music a second time, and looking directly at me, in a stern voice he said, "We'll have a little more knowledge." I felt a quiver run up my spine.

He said he didn't understand how a devotee could ever wonder, "What will happen to me, who will take care of me?" He compared it to holding ghee in our hand while crying for butter, emphasizing that if we have faith, only the best will come. "It's important to tell ourselves, this time, come what may, I will make it!'"

The power and conviction behind his direction to have faith, *come what may*, resonated in the depths of my soul. "Many teachers will show you the way, but I have come to take you all the way to the other shore," he added. I felt my consciousness waking up.

"But it's hard Gurudev, it's really hard sometimes," someone said.

"Is misery easier?" Gurudev replied. "If misery is easier, then stick with misery."

His words triggered a memory. Had I come this far on the path in another lifetime and dropped out before making it all the way, because my comfort zone was too small? An image of a woman climbing to the summit of a mountain flashed across my mind. Most people stop just before reaching the summit, because the path is so challenging, yet that's where the best view is. I didn't want to be the person who stopped just short of the summit.

Gurudev rose to leave the room, then stopped at the door and returned to his seat to share a story he remembered.

"There is a story about Krishna and one of his devotees," he said. "One evening, Krishna was eating dinner, when he suddenly arose to attend to a devotee who had been crying for him all day. The Gopis implored Krishna to finish his dinner before going, but Krishna couldn't be stopped. He said his devotee had been calling him all day and he had to go. However, just as Krishna was about to go out the door, he suddenly returned to the dinner table. He sat down and began eating his dinner, explaining that the devotee had decided to pray to someone else, which just gave him more time to finish eating."

Nature is very intelligent. It knows just what you need and when you need it. I'll never know if Gurudev had set the situation up the way it unfolded in order to push my buttons, or if the situation had presented itself so that he could teach me. Either way, it brought me to a point where I had to stop and reflect on what it was I wanted for my life, and what I was willing to forbear in order to have it.

I went back to my room and unpacked my suitcases.

The next morning, I was up and ready very early for another trip to the United Nations. The Ashram was completely silent at such an early hour, but I wanted to pay my respects to Gurudev before leaving. And so, tiptoeing in stocking feet down a long, dimly lit hallway toward his suite, I bowed in front of his door. With my head bent in a prayer of gratitude, the door slowly opened and to my surprise, I looked up to see Gurudev smiling at me. We said our goodbyes, and I skipped down the hall with renewed faith and commitment, toward the next extraordinary chapter of my journey.

Becoming a full-time teacher on this path required calling up inner strength and capacities that I never knew I had. It would also bring me to the height of spiritual experience, worldly luxuries as well as placing me in difficult and uncomfortable circumstances. The challenge was learning how to remain dispassionate with a genuine smile, regardless of where I landed.

I put my house up for sale, dropped my belongings and two cats off with my sister and her family in Texas, and flew to Washington, DC. Following Gurudev's direction, I moved in with a host family and got to work on organizing our first IAHV event at the National Press Club, where Gurudev was slated as the keynote speaker.

With just a handful of dedicated volunteers, we created the invitations, pulled together a high profile list of invitees, and I started knocking on embassy doors. One afternoon, by the time I had finished walking up and down embassy row, I'd said my own name along with the name of our foundation so many times my tongue was twisting! The anticipated day arrived. I stood behind the curtain waiting for my turn at the podium when Gurudev walked over.

"Are you nervous, Patti?"

"Absolutely," I replied.

In his own way, he gave me a big vote of confidence, which was just the boost I needed. As I walked to the stage, I felt clear and confident addressing the crowd of dignitaries, before inviting Gurudev to the stage. Later that afternoon, Gurudev addressed a gathering of scientists at the National Institutes of Health. Although attendance at both events wasn't as large as we'd hoped for, Gurudev encouraged us when he said that many seeds had been planted, which would one day sprout.

That evening, almost two hundred devotees gathered in Neelam and Vinod's home for a *satsang* with Gurudev. And just like a dream, the events of the day, along with all the ups and downs of organizing the event in just six weeks, washed away, making room to enjoy the present moment.

The next week, I was told that I had to move from my home in DC. My house in Denver had sold, so I had nowhere to go. I called Gurudev, crying. He simply said that it would all work out and that we would speak again in a month. My friend Ann invited the cats and me to live with her, so back I went to Texas. The familiarity of my old neighborhood and friends was comforting at first, but it didn't last long. I'd outgrown my old way of life and knew that it was just a matter of time before I would move on.

A few months later, I was back in Germany at our Ashram. One afternoon, a few of us went with Gurudev for a ride to a nearby town in Switzerland. I'd noticed for a while now that whenever Gurudev traveled from one city or town to another, the sun came out, as if to greet him.

It was a gray day in Germany that afternoon, and I smiled when the sun came out the moment we crossed the border into Switzerland.

Gurudev suggested we stop to see the water along the way. No one knew the directions and GPS didn't exist at the time, so he directed us to a lake. It was absolutely amazing watching him walk unnoticed through the quaint European village, a saint from another time in long white silk robes and black hair waving in the breeze, while chil-

Basel, Switzerland.

dren played on cobblestone streets. I've never understood how sometimes he can't move an inch without thousands of people pulling and tugging at him, and at other times, it's as though no one sees him at all.

We remained at the pier while he walked the strand on his own. When he returned, I made a joke about the old iron rings on the pier, used for tying up boats. I said, "Do you use this for tying up bad devotees?" He laughed and said, bad devotees tie themselves up! On a more serious note, I continued, "Gurudev, your work is so important, and I wonder, are we (meaning myself) really the best you can get to do this important work? It feels like we're not making progress very quickly and we (I) are making a lot of mistakes along the way."

"One by one, Patti," said Gurudev. "We uplift, one by one. The fire is still there. All you have to do is blow the ashes away; the fire is still burning. Some ash gets accumulated over the mind, but once you blow the ash away, the fire will rise up and shine brightly. Don't sit and brood over anything. Just march ahead knowing that you are fire and that you have all the blessings and that only the best will happen."

Although Gurudev didn't eat sugar, he knew what a treat ice cream was for us. I waited in the tiny car with him, along with another devotee while another person got the ice cream. Across the street, a bus full of people had been waiting at a traffic light for quite a long time. "Not one person in that bus is smiling. Not one," said Gurudev. I'd noticed the same thing whenever I waited for a bus in Geneva—people didn't make eye contact and generally looked quite serious. It gave me an idea.

"Excuse me, Gurudev," I said, stretching forward from the back seat to roll open the sunroof.

"Patti, the police will come."

"Well, you are the Guru after all, so that's your job!" I cheerfully replied as I stood up to wave at the people on the bus through the sunroof. People looked, but not one person cracked even a hint of a smile. I was determined to see at least one person smile or wave before I sat back down. Gurudev laughed and laughed, and we all cheered when finally, one timid woman dressed all in black cracked a little smile and waved back.

Gurudev shared the story in *satsang* that evening, and for the rest of the week. Soon after, he launched Laughing Clubs throughout Europe. When a film crew came to interview us about the success of the clubs, they laughed so much that they were literally falling off of their film trolleys.

My friend Ann called me at the Ashram. My older cat had gotten into a fight with her cat and had bitten her finger, which had become infected. She was shocked to discover that her doctor had called the authorities to report the bite, even though the pet belonged to our home. My cat was confined to "Kitty-Jail," at our local veterinarian's office. I knew that it was time to find my cats another home. I hung up, distraught over the idea of having to give my pets away after caring for them for twelve years. They were my last connection to my former life. I started crying and didn't stop throughout the entire *satsang*. I was speaking with my friend Shirley about the situation when Gurudev passed us in the hallway. I'd been trying to find a place for my pets for six months and kept hitting a brick wall. There was no way I could even think about placing them in a shelter. "She just wants a good home for the cats, so that they can stay together as they age," Shirley said to Gurudev. He listened attentively and said it was time to let the cats go.

And just like that, the next morning, all my worries were over. A friend called to say that she would happily take them both in. By the time I returned to Texas, I was completely unattached in every way possible and moving forward, like fire.

Time and again, Gurudev takes care of the subtle. This same trip when he first arrived at the Ashram, it was December and very cold. The heat had gone out in the entire building the night before, and no one had been able to figure out what was wrong. The building was very big and very old, and we didn't really have the money to pay an electrician. No one knew what to do. Within minutes of his arrival, Gurudev was made aware of the situation. He instructed the people who had been working on the heater to go back down to the basement and to do their best one more time. Shrugging their shoulders, they left the room thinking the Guru just didn't understand the depth of the situation. Ten minutes later, however, they called full of excitement—the heat was now working throughout the building. They didn't know how it was working, because they didn't do more than jiggle the same knobs they'd tried earlier that day. "Gurudev, how did that happen?" I asked him, knowing it was his hand at work. He just smiled and winked, mischievously.

from luxury **to laundry**

I'd heard Gurudev give a wonderful knowledge talk about rising above the opposites in life and moving beyond all the paradoxes in order to be at peace with what is. This, he said, is key to maintaining peace of mind and I was learning the value of this wisdom.

I was no longer traveling in first class, which I was accustomed to after working for an airline. Now, I was cramped in economy class and sticking my fingers in my ears to drown out the piercing cries of unhappy babies. All the flavors of life are present when traveling and teaching, especially abroad. I've shed my fair share of tears, wallowed in anger, seethed in frustration and thought many a time that I wasn't cut out for this kind of life, but in the end, following Gurudev's commitment to uplifting society, I stayed the course. Stories of his early travels abroad inspired me to use every situation I faced as an opportunity to apply the knowledge.

Know that the Divine is taking care.

Life is found to be caught up in storms so very often. You are not yourself when you are in a storm. At those moments all your spiritual practices, concepts, ideas and ideals fall apart. Your devotion, love and all the beautiful things you cherish in your life, simply don't seem to be there or mean anything. A whirlwind rises in you and throws you off balance.

What do you do? The first thing to do is to become aware of this. At that moment, the storm will subside and you will find some relief. Stop resisting the storm. Take it, gulp it in its totality; go deep into it and you will see it is nothing. Every storm that has come into your life has widened your horizon, has made you deep and more powerful. Every storm has destroyed some smallness in you. Know that there is a power, some power, someone who is really caring for you.

—Sri Sri Ravi Shankar

When he first began traveling around the world, people didn't know how to care for a Guru. During one of his earliest visits to Japan, the room he was given was so dirty that he had to clean the tub and shower curtain himself before using it. The next morning, when a devotee traveling with him saw how filthy the room was, she wanted to move him to a hotel room. "If we don't leave it cleaner than we found it, then how will they ever learn?" he said. "It is our responsibility to clean it, and in doing so, we teach." The Guru imparts the knowledge in every moment, whether through words, actions, or silence.

I've come across all kinds of situations while traveling and teaching. I've stayed in seven-star hotels and also have had to clean dirty bathroom sinks in people's homes before I could wash my face. I've enjoyed delicious food on expensive china and I've had to sweep up dead roaches in a dirty kitchen before I ate. I've worked with people who were extraordinarily creative and easy to collaborate with, and I've worked with the most unreasonable and difficult personalities. If I wanted to enjoy peace of mind as a way of life from now on, I had to learn how to shake hands with disturbance.

Gurudev returned to the USA and I met up with him in Seattle, where he'd sent me to teach a few months earlier. From there, our small caravan drove with him to Portland, Oregon, before continuing on to Lake Tahoe for Guru Purnima. Like many of us Westerners in those early days, our hosts didn't know how to care for a Guru. When my friend Susannah and I saw the food being prepared for Gurudev, we knew it wasn't suitable and requested permission to cook for him. While cooking for Gurudev is a huge honor, it was also a very big stretch, since neither of us were proficient cooks. Susannah and I took great joy in getting all kinds of fresh organic vegetables, grains and different foods, although we had no idea what to prepare. In the end, Gurudev took over the kitchen.

I chopped the vegetables while he prepared the spaghetti sauce. Working in silence with Gurudev in the kitchen was a lesson in awareness. He moved about the kitchen as though he'd cooked there all of his life, while I did my best to anticipate his every need from handing him a napkin to placing the oregano in his hands the precise moment it was required. When he decided to add some Indian spices to the spaghetti sauce, I held my breath, wondering what my Italian ancestors would think about that!

Once everything was ready, I carefully placed the meal on a silver tray, praying with all my might that I would be able to serve him without spilling a drop of red sauce on his white silk robes!

Just prior to meeting up with Gurudev, I had gone through a confusing and upsetting time. Still accustomed to a lavish corporate lifestyle, I was having a difficult time adjusting to life on a small stipend. Just before I left for Seattle, our Board sent a message that caused me to begin worrying about finances. Not only would they no longer cover my expenses, it was decided that they were going to terminate my stipend as well. Going forward, it was up to me to not only fund my salary but everything to do with the organization I headed up as well. The news came as a shock.

The policy change felt very unjust, and I tried reaching Gurudev to find out what was actually going on. He was unreachable for weeks, so until I could meet with him, I watched one knowledge video after another to help me cope. I finally had a chance to speak with him after lunch that day. He chided me about getting upset and losing so much time and energy over the situation. "You were going to see me in a matter of months," he said. "Something would have worked out."

A few days later, a small group of us flew with Gurudev to Lake Tahoe for Guru Purnima. Disappointed for not having more faith in myself, let alone a higher power, I was uncharacteristically quiet, standing next to Gurudev as we waited for our luggage. "This is your first Guru Purnima, isn't it?" he asked. I nodded my head yes. "Guru Purnima is celebrated to remind you that you are the light of the world and for the world. There is no good light and bad light. Light is light! Don't be so serious Patti. Be light!"

In accordance with the Vedic tradition, Guru Purnima takes place on the fullest day of the moon in July, and it's a very auspicious day for spiritual seekers. Guru Purnima is the day a seeker reflects on the wisdom that life has offered and how much he or she has grown in knowledge. It's a day of gratitude, devotion and celebration. A unique quality of Gurudev's is how much he makes himself available day in and out to everyone on this planet. There have been a number of times when in deep and sincere prayer, I've asked for a sign that I was being heard by the

Divine, and that very day, I smelled jasmine in the middle of a Colorado winter or the undeniable aroma of incense spontaneously filled the house.

Guru Purnima.

All kinds of people from around the world come to celebrate in his presence during Guru Purnima, including devotees and Swamis from other traditions. One Swami in particular was bowled over by how fortunate Gurudev's devotees are when he saw how much care was being given to each and every person, to ensure their continued progress on the path. "You all are very lucky," said Swamiji. Sri Sri has paved the path for you all, so after a slap don't forget you are sitting in his lap."

Some years, Gurudev will go for a walk at midnight on Guru Purnima, or we'll follow him to the highest point at the Ashram to see the full moon while a wooden flute softly plays. At the Canadian Ashram, he might take a midnight ride on a raft shaped like our logo of two swans (a symbol of non-violence). He is completely spontaneous. As soon as the door to his *kutir* opens, to everyone's delight, he walks toward the midnight destination with the speed and bounce of a teenager.

The experience of being on the lake with Gurudev, under the light of a full moon is rare. At these times, it's as though nothing else in the world exists. Until, that is, the peaceful environment is disturbed by the sound of over-zealous devotees jumping into the lake and swimming over to the float, in order to get closer to the Guru. This happens more often than not these days, and I can't even count the number of times the raft almost sank, dumping everyone including the Guru into the cold water!

austin or boston:
learning to trust

I was back in Dallas preparing for Gurudev's upcoming visit and eager to see him again. The event was low-key but well attended. The day before he was scheduled to return to India, he called me in to watch a news report with him and a few others. The journalist was reporting on a growing trend toward spirituality among US college students. Unbeknownst to me at the time, the report was also a foreshadowing of my next assignment. Before leaving the room, I requested an appointment with Gurudev, to which he replied, "You can have the first appointment tomorrow."

The following morning, I knocked on his door about 10:00 a.m., which is when meetings usually start. I was informed that Gurudev was meditating, so I went next door to meditate with friends. After some time, I returned to Gurudev's door and was told again that he was meditating. I returned to my friends and waited. Thirty minutes later, the phone rang. "Gurudev is calling you."

I picked up my things and bolted for his door before anyone else could beat me to it, but I hadn't taken two steps into the room when Gurudev began scolding me, "You're an executive! You are to be on time!" I looked behind me to see if he was speaking to someone else, but no one was there.

I began to explain myself in earnest.

"Patti, you are to listen now. No explanations," he said. I was still a little confused when he excused himself to take an urgent phone call. While I was waiting, I remembered hearing him speak about defense consciousness, and how it makes us small and weak, so, rather than reacting, I chose to listen and learn. When he finished the call, he instructed me to focus on bringing the knowledge to college students and suggested that I move to Boston. "Live near Cambridge University, you'll like it there," he said. The assignment and location resonated well with me. But when I let our Board know about my new plan, they informed me that I was going to Austin, not Boston. Apparently, the foundation couldn't afford an apartment for me in Boston.

I flipped out. I had my instructions from the Guru and did not intend to follow anyone else's.

On the way out the door I passed Gurudev on his way to the airport. "What is happening, Gurudev?! You told me to go to Boston and now our Board says I am going to Austin and I'm supposed to live with someone who I don't even know. What is happening?" I demanded.

Gurudev simply said, "Patti, you have got to learn to trust," before walking out the door and into a waiting car.

My pattern of leaving a situation when it became too unpleasant began to reemerge and my mind worked overtime figuring out an exit strategy. But, for now, I had no choice but to take a friend to the airport. My friend John did his best to help me to understand the value of trusting in the Divine, especially when walking the spiritual path under Gurudev's guidance, but I had no ears to listen. I was still fuming when I saw Gurudev in the departure area. The seat next to him was vacant, and I took it. Pointing to a young man from India he said, "That is Sriram. He has been asking me to send an Art of Living teacher to Austin for years. You will live with him; he's a very nice young man."

Nothing in my life had prepared me for living with someone I didn't know, even if he was a devotee; it seemed too far out of my comfort zone.

"Patti, get the college program moving in the USA. Try this out for three months, and if it doesn't work out, we'll do something different," said Gurudev, his voice full of understanding. Trust was definitely an issue for me at the time, and I didn't give it away to many people. But I trusted Gurudev completely and agreed to his request. "I'm sorry I'm so difficult, Gurudev."

"Oh Patti, you're not difficult," he said lovingly. "You are a challenge! But you're not difficult."

⁓⁓⁓⁓⁓

"What's that smell?" I shouted downstairs.

"My father is cooking curried rice; come eat," Sriram shouted back up.

It would be a few more years before I would appreciate exotic spices from India; for now, I found the smell pungent. Plugging my nose, I dialed pizza delivery.

For a lot of people in America, a visit from family lasts no more than a week. We had rented a large and beautiful home, and Sriram was, as Gurudev said, a very nice young man. But when he informed me that his father was coming for three months, I wanted to scream!

The Austin Art of Living chapter was new and we only had a handful of volunteers. This meant that for every course I taught, I was also the head of public relations, the graphic designer, treasurer, house cleaner and even the cook for all the course participants, in addition to being the teacher. One by one, we registered people for our workshops and when no one attended our free introductory seminars here and there, we practiced with one another.

I was surprised at how stressed out and unfocused college students seemed overall, and I did everything I could to inspire everyone I met to attend our Happiness course.

Starting up a new chapter meant raising funds for a center as well. Until we got to that point, we had to rely on renting a room at the university or a living room in a student apartment. I had to hold my breath the first time I visited student housing, where we planned to conduct our first workshop. Dishes and laundry were piled everywhere, and the smell of six young bachelors living together in a two-bedroom apartment was more than my senses could handle.

I had no choice but to find a way to work with what we had. So I sat the innocent and enthusiastic young volunteers down and helped them to understand that the environment needed to reflect the sacredness of the knowledge we were sharing. A few days later, our first course began with ten college students from all around the world and I gently began leading them into the first stage of the breathing techniques. A stillness came over the room as the students closed their eyes and the count began. "Breathe in, one—two—three—four." I relaxed as I guided the *pranayamas*—until I saw two huge roaches walking across the living room floor.

Once everyone left, I had another talk with my young charges. The next day with eyes full of pride, they excitedly took me from room to room to see how clean it was now. But within moments, I was coughing uncontrollably and had to step outside from the overpowering smell of insecticide. We agreed to combine our energies and intentions to find a suitable venue before the next course began.

Austin was becoming a desirable city to live in, and rental properties near the university were rising. I didn't know how we were going to find anything we could afford as a center, so out of desperation one afternoon I loaded my car up with marketing brochures and set out to find a venue, one way or the other.

Close to campus, I came across a historical looking structure, which was being used as an adult daycare facility. I met with the assistant to the Executive Director, a chubby fellow with round cheeks, kind eyes and a nice smile. He had recently moved to Austin from New York, where he had worked at the United Nations. I was pleasantly surprised when I learned that he knew about Gurudev and took it as a positive sign.

Austin, 2000.

I had to go on intuition to come up with how much we could afford every month and told him all I had was a few hundred dollars. It turned out that the Executive Director also knew of Gurudev's contributions to society and generously offered to find a room to fit our budget. Unfortunately, all of the rooms were too small, and I was just about to leave when the assistant suggested we take a look at the dining hall. A painting class for senior citizens was going on at the time, but we could look, as long as we were quiet.

I gasped when the door opened. Expecting to see a group of elderly people quietly painting ceramics or making crafts, I was surprised to see a completely naked seventy-five-year-old man posing on a stool for a life drawing class. To make an already uncomfortable situation even more awkward, before I could turn my head away, I made eye contact with one of my elderly neighbors, who was taking the class.

"What do you think of the room...will it work for you?" the assistant casually asked, as though nothing unusual was going on. *What do I think of the room?* The scene before me was more than I'd bargained for; I didn't know where to put my eyes.

"Uh, uh...I'm not sure...ummmm...I think it's ok," I stammered, as we exited the room.

As soon as we left, I asked for directions to the restroom, so as to collect myself.

"It's down the hall to the right, but be careful. It's haunted."

"It's haunted?! You mean by ghosts? Where are the ghosts?" I asked nervously.

"This building used to house a lot of widows during the Civil War, and the ghosts tend to hang out in the ladies' restroom," he replied matter of factly.

As a child, I was the "scaredy-cat" in the family, always asking my father to check under my bed, in the closet and in the basement for imaginary ghosts or anything else that could "go bump in the night."

Now, I was in a dilemma. The price was right, the people were kind and generous, the location was perfect and from what I could see of the dining hall, excluding the naked body, the room would work. But the comment about the building being haunted was disturbing, and as a fairly new teacher, I wasn't sure what to do.

At the time, not everyone had a computer at home and smart phones with Internet access didn't exist. Gurudev's office in India had email access, but it hadn't become common yet to communicate with him in this way. Nonetheless, the day had been so unusual, I decided to send a funny email to Gurudev about what had happened, intentionally leaving out the part about the place possibly being haunted.

Two weeks passed and I fretted day and night about teaching in that building; what if someone actually saw a ghost? One morning, I woke up, still unsure of what to do. I felt responsible for the students, and my tendency to second guess myself had a stronghold on me. Frustrated,

I stood in my living area in my bathrobe, blue teacup in my hand, and shook my fist to the heavens. "Once, just once, Gurudev, I'd like to know you hear my prayers!" I demanded.

In an instant, I felt a strong urge to check my email, but I shook it off, knowing full well that I wasn't expecting any important messages. Instead, I sat down to finish my breakfast, but the feeling that I was supposed to check my email persisted. It was as if something was pulling me into the office. Without another thought, I sat down at the computer, opened my email and was stunned when I saw a message from the Office of His Holiness Sri Ravi Shankar.

Dear Patti,

Gurudev says it is all right to teach in that building.

Jai Guru Dev

I stared at the computer screen in disbelief. I had not asked Gurudev anything about teaching in that building. Not one word! I'd only shared the funny story about finding the naked man in the dining room when I was scouting out rooms. Tapping the screen, I chuckled. "Oh, you're good!" I said aloud. "You are very, very good." I immediately dialed the folks in charge of the building to set up our next course.

Ten years later, while on a car trip with Gurudev in Colorado, I noticed the same thing I'd seen many times before—whenever we went from one town to another, or one country to another—the sun always came out to greet him. It happened again when we drove from Ridgeway to Telluride, in spite of being cautioned about a snowstorm in Telluride by locals who implored us not to go. Gurudev said it would be fine and off we went to take Gurudev on the gondola at the ski resort. When we arrived at the ski lift, the operators were amazed. "Wow, your timing is amazing!" they said to our little group. "The sun just came out minutes ago and the storm stopped. Up until now it had been closed down." I immediately looked at Gurudev, who just winked and smiled.

It wasn't the first time I had seen something mystical and unexplainable occur in Gurudev's presence. The next day when I set out to meet him early in the morning, the sky was dark and cloudy. But the moment he walked out of the hotel room and into the courtyard, the sun pushed through the clouds, as if on cue. All I could do was shake my head in wonder.

As our Austin chapter continued to expand, I started traveling with my students to other cities across the state to uplift and connect with our other chapters. In time, things shifted dynamically. More volunteers stepped up, my students became teachers, and our chapter was partnering with numerous cultural and civic organizations across town.

I regularly gave talks about the power of our Happiness course and was eager to share the benefits of it with anyone who was even slightly interested. In fact, one time, while I was going under an anesthetic for surgery, the anesthesiologist asked me about my work. Even then, I offered to lead a meditation for the hospital staff, just before the medicine kicked in.

I've always said that a good teacher is a good student. Along the way, I've made many mistakes as a leader, but in time, I learned. Many of my students from that time in my life have gone on to realize great success. I'm grateful to all of them for sticking with me through it all, and for all we did together to help others. It turns out that I never needed my own children to realize that I am a mother.

We continued doing more and more through all of the Art of Living Chapters in Texas, and when someone donated their home to us as a center, I had no doubt that a visit from the Guru was imminent.

the sky is falling,
the sky is falling!

My lifestyle changed dramatically after dedicating it to spiritual pursuits, and I started wondering if I'd lose some freedom as I moved toward enlightenment. Clearly, I had a few more concepts to kick to the curb. When the moment dawns, it will unfold as a state of consciousness, not a lifestyle.

The new millennium was approaching and just about everyone was concerned about what the year 2000, also known as "Y2K" would bring. The term referred to a problem in the coding of computerized systems that could create mayhem in computer networks around the world at the beginning of the year. It seemed like everyone was preparing for the worst. People were storing food, seeds, generators, and all sorts of survival items.

I joined Gurudev in Europe for a meditation retreat and to welcome the new Millennium in Italy. When I met with Gurudev, I presented him with a porcelain music box of Mother Mary and Jesus that played Ave Maria. His mother had passed away the previous month and I'd searched and searched for the perfect gift in honor of her memory. I think of *Amma* and Gurudev every time I see the music box still sitting in the glass case just outside of his room in Germany.

The day to depart for Italy arrived, and the air was filled with excitement while conversations in Polish, German, English, French, Spanish and other languages buzzed throughout the Ashram. Shouts of, "Hurry up!" and, "Where is Gurudev?" were heard throughout the grounds as we hoisted our luggage onto the buses that would take us to Tuscany.

Once everyone was settled on board, Gurudev came down to take his seat. Another teacher and I were standing downstairs in the lobby, waiting to help Gurudev to get settled onto the right bus. But when he passed a pile of dirty dishes and teacups left in the lobby on his way, he stopped.

"Where is the awareness?" he asked as he began picking up dirty dishes. We both felt that we'd let him and the Ashram staff down by not noticing this before. We joined Gurudev and began clearing the debris. "These buses will not leave until every dish is cleared, washed and put away properly. Tell everyone to get off of the buses and to get busy," said Gurudev, his arms filled with the dirty dishes of his devotees.

I'll never forget watching Gurudev early one morning in the German Ashram. He was walking alone, toward the meditation hall. I slowed my pace and stood back so as to give him space. He stopped and looked into the bathroom closest to the main meditation hall, and I heard cabinets being opened, as though he was looking for something. Inching my way closer, I saw him taking care to fill the empty paper rolls.

The Tuscan region of Italy, dotted with lush green hillsides and hugged by the sea, offers some of the most beautiful landscapes in the world. And it seemed to me that so many diverse people coming together to meditate and ring in the new millennium added even more to its beauty.

The Art of Living spiritual family is a fascinating tapestry of people from every corner of the world, and it only increases. It felt like this course brought every one of them together, although in reality it was just a few thousand. The main hall of the event, organized by an all-volunteer team, was an intense and chaotic assembly of people, languages, and activity along with a lot of excitement and heartfelt reunions. Translation headsets were being distributed in one corner, while people were renegotiating the cost of housing in another corner. Every few minutes, someone was screaming with delight at the sight of an old friend while another person was sitting in the middle of it all meditating. The details associated with planning an event for a few thousand people from forty different countries are staggering even for the most experienced organizer, and soon many helping hands were pitching in to help.

Gurudev, who enjoys teasing his devotees, started greeting me on that trip by saying, "It's a good omen to see an Old Lady in the morning!" in spite of the fact that I am two years younger than he is. I just laughed, hoping it was his way of blessing me with a long life.

Thirteen hundred people gathered for the New Millennium Course at Massa di Carrara, Tuscany. Finally, the much anticipated New Year's Eve arrived and just before sunset, Gurudev gathered several hundred of us for meditation on the shores of the Mediterranean, to watch the last sunset of the year. Along with 200 other devotees, I sat with Gurudev in front of the ocean, as my past dissolved with each wave, making room for the New Year.

What I really appreciate about Gurudev is how free he is to be himself, regardless of anyone's opinion, in every moment, and in every situation, whether he is inspiring terrorists to put down their arms, conferring with heads of state, resolving age-old conflicts between religious groups, or celebrating the New Year with his devotees. That evening, the hall exploded with cheers of celebration the moment the "Guru of Joy" walked in, wearing his traditional flowing white silks and touting large sequined sunglasses with the number 2000 stamped across the frames.

Everyone danced and sang to some rocking *bhajans*, until the moment Gurudev took his seat. "I want to tell you about a very special woman in my life," he said. As he began speaking about his mother, the room became silent as a single tear fell from his eye. Afterward, he led us into a powerful meditation. When Gurudev retired to his quarters, I joined my friends for dancing, a fireworks display, and some of the best pizza I've ever eaten.

The next morning, I awoke to the sound of church bells ringing across town announcing the New Year. Scooching up to the window sill for a better look, I cranked the large wooden window open all the way. The sun was shining as a light breeze gently caressed my cheek. It was a peaceful beginning to a new millennium, which, just as Gurudev had predicted, arrived without incident.

We continued on to Milan, where Gurudev had some important meetings and a public talk. The organizers had arranged a suite for him and his entourage; however, there were no hotel rooms for the rest of us. Gurudev wanted us to bunk with some of the others, but they were all so tired that we left to find our own accommodations. Every hotel was either full or too expensive. It was after midnight and we needed a room. My friend Marcy and I said a prayer for help and the next hotel we went to not only had a vacancy, it fit our budget and was just a short walk to Gurudev's hotel. Walking with him the next day, I took the opportunity to ask a question that had been on my mind for quite a while.

"How is it that we come to find a Guru; how does it work?" I said.

He just smiled, but when we got to his meeting room, he led an impromptu knowledge session for our small group, citing six reasons to be with a Guru.

1. *You want your wishes fulfilled.*

2. *Everything else looks more painful.*

3. *You want to evolve and to become enlightened.*

4. *You have a vision or goal that you share with the Guru.*

5. *You are there just to serve and give comfort to the Guru.*

6. *You belong to the Guru, there is no choice.*

Afterward, he left to do other work while we slipped out for a cappuccino to discuss which category we thought we fit into and why.

what doesn't kill you
makes you stronger

I became ill after returning from Europe and was diagnosed with mononucleosis. It seemed odd to have contracted what's popularly known as the "kissing disease," when the only romance I experienced anymore was in the movies! People teased me a lot, but the truth was that the fatigue was affecting my ability to teach or do much else. Still, as the leader and only teacher of a new chapter, I continued dragging myself out of bed and into the classroom.

A few months later, when the doctors still couldn't determine why the illness was lingering, I wondered if I should stop teaching for a while and called Gurudev. He felt that the best thing for me was to stay in the grace through teaching. "You're just going to watch television anyway, which drains your energy," he said. Just before we hung up, he told me to meet him in New York in a few weeks and to take an appointment with a world famous Ayurvedic physician who was traveling with him.

I landed at La Guardia airport and, hopping into a taxi, I arrived at the hotel where Gurudev was staying, just in time to welcome him. As he entered the hotel, I eagerly awaited his familiar smile of recognition. However, without so much as a wave, he walked past me toward the elevator.

Dismissing the brush-off, I stood by his side as he waited for the elevator doors to open. After what felt like a long, awkward silence, he asked, "Patti, have you taken the DSN course?" DSN stands for *Divya Samaj Nirman* in Sanskrit. The English translation is Dynamism for Self and Nation.

The new personality development workshop that he'd created was gaining a positive reputation as a sort of spiritual boot camp. "No I haven't," I said, wondering why he'd even brought it up since I was in New York to find a solution to my lingering illness. "Ah, you should take it!" he replied enthusiastically, before the elevator doors opened and whisked him away.

The next day, I had an appointment with the Ayurvedic doctor. However, to my disappointment, he wasn't able to make the trip and had sent his son instead, who was also an Ayurvedic physician. It's said that an authentic Ayurvedic doctor can heal just through pulse diagnosis, so I had high hopes. Unlike his father, this man had no bedside manner and when he didn't even mention the mononucleosis, I was put off. He did, however, inquire about my thyroid as he handed me a long list of Ayurvedic herbs to purchase. The consultation was over in five minutes.

When the Guru wants to dissolve something small inside of his student, he does it with precise skill. No matter how much I tried to see Gurudev the rest of the weekend, nothing worked out. The final straw was when all of the full-time faculty, except me, were invited to a private event with Gurudev. That night, alone in a friend's apartment on the Lower East-Side, I sat on the floor eating a cold slice of pizza, wondering what to do next. The whole trip seemed like a waste of energy, time and money. I certainly didn't feel very enlightened; in fact, the whole idea seemed like a fairy tale.

Gurudev was leaving for Europe the next day, and in spite of a heavy heart, I showed up to see him off. Just as the entire weekend had gone, he chatted in a friendly manner with the small group of devotees gathered, while I felt invisible. Confused as to why he had told me to even come to New York, I was reeling in my own pity party.

The ego may be the least understood level of our existence. On one hand, it's needed to encourage ourselves when we don't know our own capacity. Other than that, it's best to keep the ego in your pocket, but mine didn't want to stay there. Just when I needed to be centered and unfazed by the events happening around me, my ego whispered, "Hey, what about me? Talk to me! I am here. Look at me!"

The mind is tricky, and until my consciousness was free of duality—likes, dislikes, craving and aversions—it was going to wreak havoc on my inner peace and joy. This experience is called "*tapas*" in Sanskrit, which means our negative emotions have had their way with us and we're cooking in the juices of our own mind. *Tapas* is necessary on the path to liberation. It brings endurance and acceptance with the opposites, so that you can become unshakeable. No doubt I was in *tapas*.

To have a Guru who is able to take you all the way to enlightenment is very rare and only for the brave. A *Satguru* doesn't simply stuff his devotee with knowledge; he kindles life force and invokes intelligence, not just intellect. Which may help to explain why people the world over want to be in Gurudev's presence as often and for as long as possible. It's intoxicating.

Gurudev eventually went up to his room. I sat down with a few friends and shared my concerns about how popular he was becoming around the world. I was starting to worry about how difficult it might become to have quality time with him. Wiping tears of longing away, I sat down for *sādhanā*. When my eyes opened, I was refreshed and free of all the emotions I'd been holding onto since arriving in New York...which meant my funny bone was waking up, too.

One of our teachers, who had a habit of making up stories in order to be near Gurudev, was taking requests for personal appointments with him. Aware that this was just a ploy, I decided to have a little fun. Grabbing a stack of paper, I followed him around the room, inviting people to place their name on "my list" which would in turn put them on "his list." Everyone was laughing, except the man with the clipboard, who clearly wasn't amused.

Finally free of me, he breathed a sigh of relief when Gurudev called me in to meet with him. I thought I had wanted to speak to Gurudev about my health situation, but instead what came out was longing to spend more time with him. "You are becoming so well-known and time with you is more and more rare. How will I manage as the years pass?" I asked with tears in my eyes.

Gurudev often says that his teachers are not only his limbs, they are his very soul. "Know that you are one of my very limbs," he said, holding out his thumb. I don't remember what followed after that. I just remember walking out of the room filled with an inexplicable sense of gratitude, as though I'd just been wrapped in a blanket of benevolence. Months later, reflecting on that moment, I struggled to recall whose thumb I had actually looked at. Was it his or mine? I could still see and feel the warmth and color of the thumb and see the fabric of the skin, as though it was right in front of me. Was this the experience of oneness that the ancient scriptures spoke of?

Gurudev left and I stayed back to attend the course even though I wasn't sure that I'd be able to make it through to the end. The teacher was very understanding and assured me that I could rest at any point, as needed. "It's best you just be here, do what you can and be in the grace," he said. I immersed myself into the knowledge and was able to participate in every process, including showing up early in the morning and staying in class until late at night. I was enjoying the course and had forgotten all about being ill. By the time the course finished, I was free of several deep impressions that had chipped away at my self-confidence and sense of security my entire life. I left New York energized and ready to move forward without a trace of fatigue.

It was clear that the whole weekend had been a setup to help me heal emotionally and physically.

My doctor was completely baffled the following week when my checkup revealed no signs of mononucleosis. Life hummed along after that, with more and more people attending my courses than ever before. As our work blossomed and expanded throughout the state, there was no doubt that a visit from the Guru was just around the corner.

we don't believe in miracles;
we count on them

Gurudev's office confirmed that he would visit Austin on his next USA tour. Our volunteers immediately booked the largest and most prestigious hall available, at the University of Texas. Gurudev had become much more well-known by now. Yet, I was a little concerned about our ability to fill such a large auditorium along with organizing a meditation retreat for five hundred people.

Organizing any large event is wrought with challenges, but doing it with only volunteers required me to take my leadership and organizational skills to a whole new level. Once again, we didn't have much money in our account, the timeline was short, and our volunteer staff worked elsewhere during the day. On the other hand, I also knew what an impact organizing an event of this magnitude for the first time would have on my students' growth, not only spiritually but as leaders. So taking a collective breath in and moving on faith, we got to work. Day in and day out, we took care of endless details and accommodated the varying needs of the people coming to our city while giving introductory talks and meeting with leaders from every cultural, civic, government, and business group in town.

Everything was moving along well, when a few weeks before the event, I received a cryptic email from Gurudev's office. The message simply said that he would not meet with anyone but devotees during his upcoming visit to Austin. Puzzled, I contacted one of our Board members who was equally confused. I then contacted Gurudev's office directly to find out what this was about and was advised that he was in Delhi at an event for hundreds of thousands of people. They did their best to deliver the message, but by the time the office reached Gurudev, it was too late. He'd gone into silence for the next ten days.

The situation created quite a dilemma. If we continued to promote the public talk and it wasn't going to happen, we would risk our reputation, along with throwing money out the window. With no way to reach Gurudev to clarify whether or not the message had been sent in error, it was on my shoulders to make a decision. After conferring with our Board and key volunteers, I canceled the event and did my best to re-inspire and redirect the rest of the team. The next day, we reserved a boat large enough to hold 200 people and started making calls to our membership base across the state to update them on the changes.

Many of the people who planned to travel to Austin were upset, and others even went so far as to place doubt on our intentions. They demanded explanations that I just didn't have. The following week, after hanging up from yet another upset volunteer, my phone rang. A youthful sounding voice on the other end casually said, "Hi Patti, what are you doing?" I had no idea who was calling and asked for his name. When he just repeated, "What are you doing?" I realized it was Gurudev! "Well Gurudev, the truth is, I never understood the cryptic message I got from your office telling me that you only wanted to meet with devotees. I couldn't reach you and we ended up canceling all the events. I just hung up with yet another person who thinks I am either lying or trying to cover something up!"

He started laughing. "Patti, I was thinking...why don't we hold a public talk there after all? What do you think?" My stomach did a back-flip; he was scheduled to arrive in less than two weeks.

Laying my head down on my desk in exasperation, I said, "I don't understand what's happening. What do you want, Gurudev? We had the best hall in town and canceled it. Next, we reserved a large boat for a devotee-only event and it took a lot to inspire everyone to get on board with that. Now you say we should go back to a public event.

Please just tell me what you want, Gurudev, and I'll do that. Whatever you want, I just need to know what that is."

"To create chaos?" he said, laughing even harder this time. I assured him that he'd done a great job in that capacity; in fact, an excellent job!

"Patti, see about a venue that seats about 300 people in an upscale neighborhood, maybe at a church or something like that. *Jai Guru Dev!*"

I was so baffled by the turn of events that I carefully considered my next move. Nervously dialing my strongest volunteer, I crossed my fingers that she would be able to get on the same page with me. My plan was to find a venue within twenty-four hours, before sharing the latest change in plans with everyone else. Before going to bed, I read some knowledge by Gurudev: *"We need to make our base in knowledge very strong. It is knowledge that helps us move through chaos with a smile. There is abundant chaos in the world, so if you want to keep your smile, then you have to be well-founded in knowledge."*

The next morning, applying Gurudev's motto, which is to "make the impossible, possible," we searched the Internet for anything that was even remotely similar to what he'd described over the phone.

Phone call after phone call ended in disappointment. Austin is not a very big city and available rental halls at the last minute were few and far between. But we were determined to find the proverbial needle in the haystack. Toward the end of the day, I came across a venue that I'd never heard of. It was located in the most upscale part of town, offered a stunning view of the surrounding hills and countryside, and its architecture was reflective of an old Spanish mission. The cathedral-looking doors opened into an elegant courtyard that led to a 300-person theatre.

Was this the church in the upscale neighborhood that Gurudev had described?

Devotees often say, "We don't believe in miracles in the Art of Living—we count on them!" I crossed my fingers that I'd just found our miracle.

When we called, I was told that the venue was sold out for months, and the cost was way over our budget. There was no doubt in my mind that this was the very place Gurudev had described, and with no other option on the table, we asked them to call us back if something canceled. Then we prayed. An hour later, a very surprised event manager called to say that someone had just canceled and the date we wanted was ours; we had to bring them a deposit that evening.

We immediately drove to the venue and signed a contract. To cover our costs, we'd have to sell the place out. That evening, our entire team meditated together and got into action sending out invitations, arranging media interviews, coordinating ticket sales and managing event logistics. Two weeks later, Gurudev was presented on stage with a proclamation from the mayor, declaring January tenth as Sri Sri Ravi Shankar Day in Austin, Texas, to a sold-out audience.

Not too long after this, the warning about my thyroid that the Ayurvedic doctor had given me in New York came to light. I ended up having surgery to remove a goiter, which I prayed wasn't cancerous. The night before the surgery, Gurudev called to assure me that there was no cancer. When I told him that I wouldn't be able to speak for at least twenty-four hours, he joked that this would be a big relief to the world, which made me laugh! It was a welcome relief in the face of a serious situation.

The day of the operation my mother was with me, along with my younger sister and her two small children. True to Gurudev's prediction, there was no cancer. A few weeks later, I appeared stable and my family returned to their homes. But something had gone haywire in my system and the very next morning I had to take myself to the emergency room. Every time I stood, my blood pressure dropped to a dangerous level and I was losing a lot of blood. I was admitted to the hospital and my sister turned her car around to stay with me. The doctor was concerned and put me on a morphine drip to lessen the pain. I began wondering if this was my last night on earth and called a student to bring in a cassette recorder so that I could listen to Vedic chants while someone dialed Gurudev.

Gurudev reassured me that I would be all right. Physical circumstances didn't allow surgery at the moment, and I was released with a promise to see a specialist within twenty-four hours. Things didn't improve and a week later,

I was back for another operation. By now, my energy levels were plummeting, when Gurudev called from Canada to see how I was doing. "Just be cheerful now, Patti. You'll heal better and faster that way. I just want you to be Badda Bing, Badda Boom!"

The second surgery didn't address the issue, and I ended up having a third surgery to correct the problem. When Gurudev called later that week, I was at my lowest point. "Gurudev, I feel very low now. I'm sorry, I don't feel cheerful about anything. I am so tired, and it hurts a lot." What he said next lit a firecracker under me. "Well, you're going to die in a few years anyway."

"A few more years! What does *that* mean?!" I exclaimed as my energy rose up.

"How many do you want?" Gurudev calmly asked.

"How many more are you going to be here?" I replied.

He laughed. "Oh, Patti, there are so many more interesting dimensions in life. I will show you," he said, and with a quick, *Jai Guru Dev*, he was off the phone. With just a few words from Gurudev, I realized how much I wanted to live. Guru Purnima was coming up in a few weeks, and I wanted to attend so that I could finish healing completely. After checking with my surgeon, I got the ok to travel, as long as I rested daily and used a wheelchair. I sent a note to Gurudev, requesting his blessings to see that I made it safely to Guru Purnima. Two weeks later, to the amazement of my friends and family, I was in Lake Tahoe where the celebration was taking place. When I saw Gurudev, I asked him why I was going through one health crisis after another. "Do not create more karma by asking this question. Asking why only perpetuates karma," he said, while handing me his emails to read. Every single email I read was from someone seeking his blessings due to a cancer they or a family member were suffering from. By the time I read the third letter, I looked up at him and with a voice full of gratitude, I said, "I got it. Thank you."

I had a wonderful time in Lake Tahoe, rested well, and meditated a lot. By the time I returned to Texas, I was healthier with more energy than I'd known in years.

sacred rituals and
a sense of mischief

My friends used to joke about the incredible number of yellow sticky notes on my cupboards, but my system worked. Any and every task that popped into my mind, whether it was today or in six months was written down on a yellow sticky note. Every time a task was completed, a note was removed and I felt satisfied. Along with many pads of yellow sticky notes, I always had a long list of questions for Gurudev, whether it was about the path or something I was working on that I felt needed his input or approval.

During one tour, I had been pursuing him for days to get answers about a project I was working on. Finally, on the last night after a very long day of endless meetings and events, a few of us were watching the news with him. When I pushed one more time to get my answers, Gurudev turned his chair completely away from me to face the television and said, "You can ask your questions during commercials."

Completely oblivious and focused only on what I wanted, I completely missed the sign to put away my list and just relax. In fact, earlier that year, still clinging to the need for perfection, I'd asked him what I needed to improve on. "Just relax," he replied. My feverishness to push for answers to my questions brought the evening to a quick close. A friend took me aside. "Never push your own agenda around a Guru. Just be in his presence and if there is something you really need to ask, just keep a slight intention. Everything will come to you in due time."

A few years later, I was back in Germany to attend one of the first Guru *Puja* courses with Gurudev's sister, Bhanu. Guru *Puja* is a sacred ritual in honor of the Holy Tradition of Vedic Masters who have passed the knowledge down to us.

Gurudev arrived a few days before the course, which made for a more laid back environment. After *satsang* each evening, a small group of us watched the old *I Love Lucy* comedy shows with him, roaring with laughter.

Not too many years earlier, I'd sent my entire collection of The *I Love Lucy* Show—150-plus episodes—to him at the Canadian Ashram. When he opened them, he sent a message:

*You have sent me so many I Love Lucy
tapes, I have to take one more incarnation
to watch all those tapes!*

*Love and Blessings,
Gurudev*

Chanting the Guru *Puja* takes one to a very high state of consciousness and repeating it for hours left me in total bliss, in spite of struggling with the Sanskrit. Bhanu, who is a Sanskrit scholar, delicately explained each line of the ancient chant as though she was opening up every petal of a delicate lotus blossom. The stories she shared about growing up with Gurudev always left me in awe and wanting for more. At the same time, knowing Gurudev was just upstairs and accessible while I was sitting for long hours in a classroom was wreaking havoc with my commitment.

So when a friend from Croatia, who hadn't seen Gurudev in a year, sat next to me during the last hours on the last day of the course I seized the opportunity. "Let's go to Gurudev before everyone lines up at his door in the next hour when class lets out." My friend agreed, and out the classroom and up the stairs we went. I was surprised but not shocked to see two of our fellow classmates in the room already. One of them is a business professional and the other a researcher, but from the looks on their faces you would have thought that I'd just caught two middle-schoolers playing hooky! Tipping my head to my fellow students, I took a seat.

Gurudev was looking out the window at the old farmer and his wife who lived next door, commenting on how hard they worked and how much they accomplished at their age. Their garden was full of pumpkins of every size and shape and pointing at me, he joked, "Those pumpkins have more *prana* than Montella!" to which I rolled my eyes while everyone enjoyed a good laugh. "Come, let's go!" he then said. Happy to be going for a walk with him in the fresh air, I took the good-natured teasing in stride.

Uncharacteristically, he left the building down the fire escape stairs, just outside of his suite, rather than walking through the main building and out the front door. Since his usual route would have taken us too close to the classroom for my comfort, it worked for me. Our Ashram is made up of several large buildings, joined by long hallways with windows. It's sort of like a U shape, which meant that the hill that we were walking on with Gurudev was directly across from the classroom.

Unfortunately, I didn't notice this at first. What I did notice was that rather than walking forward with a spring in his step as he usually does, Gurudev kept walking back and forth on top of the hill as though he was trying to decide which path to take.

After a few minutes going back and forth like this, all of a sudden he took a sharp turn to the right, heading down the hill and toward the windows in my classroom. Anyone who was looking out of my classroom window had a full view of us up on that hill. Grabbing my friend's hand, I shouted, "*Run!*" Just then, I saw Gurudev walking up to the classroom window and heard him say, "Bhanu, aren't you missing a student? Where's Montella?"

I knew the Ashram well and shouted directional commands to my friends as we wound our way downstairs, through halls and around corners. I was as intent as ever to make my way through the huge building, in order to meet up with Gurudev on the other side. I lost a few of them along the way, as they didn't want to be caught out of class, but I kept going. I reached the other side of the Ashram and ran to catch up to Gurudev, when someone, who was standing behind Gurudev, started frantically waving his arms and silently mouthing, "*Stop!*" But I kept running, so as not to miss the walk. As soon as Gurudev turned and saw me coming, he told me to stop and return to class.

I don't know what came over me, but class was almost over and I had really worked hard to get this far. So I kept running toward Gurudev. As I moved closer, he put his hand up and told me, again, to return to class, then he looked toward the windows of the classroom. That's when I saw 300 pairs of eyes watching the scene outside and at least three people climbing out the window to join us.

I froze. "Patti, return to class right now or I will fail you," said Gurudev in a no-nonsense tone.

Not only did I not want to be responsible for completely disrupting Bhanu's classroom, having my own Guru give me a failing grade for a workshop that called in the entire Holy Tradition was not good karma! Defeated, I returned to class while Gurudev continued his walk.

a critical time
for the world

The start of a New Year holds much hope with the past behind us and a future of possibilities.

Being with Gurudev during this time guarantees a joy-filled *satsang*, knowledge and deep meditation. One year, just before the fireworks were set to take off, I was part of what we affectionately called, "a Guru Great Escape," which meant a few devotees had cooked up a plan to whisk Gurudev away for some fun. If you were very skillful and he didn't have any pressing appointments, you might just get away with it.

On New Year's Eve in Germany, as Gurudev was walking out of the hall, a few of us whisked him away to see the fireworks in the town of Baden Baden, about an hour away. As we drove through small villages, Gurudev commented that only the remains of bottle rockets and streamers littered the streets, indicating the farmers were already fast asleep in bed. We assured him that even though the villagers had celebrated early, there would be a big fireworks display in Baden Baden. Our friend drove as fast as he could, in order to make it on time. We were almost at our destination when we heard the sound of fireworks just as our car entered a long tunnel. Everyone was ready to jump out of the car as soon as we arrived, but by the time we exited the tunnel, the show was over. We were embarrassed about what had just happened, but Gurudev just laughed and laughed and we headed back to the Ashram.

No one had any idea at the start of the New Year just how much the world was about to change.

On September 11, 2001, four United States passenger planes were hijacked by al-Qaeda terrorists. Two of the planes intentionally crashed into both towers of the World Trade Center in New York City. Less than two hours later, both towers collapsed, killing thousands of people and injuring thousands more. A third plane crashed into the Pentagon, and the building partially collapsed. The fourth plane was steered toward Washington, DC, but crashed into a field when courageous passengers overcame the hijackers.

That morning, as the nightmare was unfolding, one of my students called crying hysterically. Turning on the television, along with the rest of the country, I watched in horror as people fell to their death in a vain attempt to escape the burning towers. This was the deadliest terror attack in world history, and the country went into a nationwide panic.

No one knew what was happening or if more attacks were imminent and how they would be carried out.

Within hours, businesses boarded up, gas stations ran out of fuel and children hurried home from school while the streets and highways emptied. It was a confusing and frightening time.

That evening, I gathered my students to meditate and pray for the deceased and their families, for our country, and for the world. Later that night, Gurudev sent a message to his teachers:

Be Brave. We have to face a new era and bring common sense to society. This tragedy is reminding us of our greater task and the urgency to be more active in the world and to bring this knowledge and common sense to all those who believe in destruction and violence. At this moment, only inner strength and prayer will help.

Let everyone around the world meditate and do satsang. *No place in the world will be safe if common sense and* satsang *are not brought to every corner of the*

planet. Let every local satsang *plan group
meditations and* satsangs *that are open
to the public. Invite all your friends. Only
meditation can bring harmony in this world.*

Jai Guru Dev,
Gurudev

Art of Living volunteers, many of whom were victims
of the attack themselves, got into action at Ground Zero,
within hours. They arrived at firehouses with duffel bags
filled with sandwiches for hundreds of first responders
who were exhausted and hadn't eaten for hours. Our
foundation led meditations and conducted free trauma
relief workshops across the country, for anyone impacted
by the terror attack. That week, along with student groups
of different faiths and cultures, we marched for peace at
the University of Texas in Austin and I led a meditation.
As life would have it, this was just the first of many peace
vigils I would lead for years to come.

Thousands of people, including one of my own rel-
atives and members of my American Airlines family,
suffered during and after the terror attack. It was an
unprecedented crisis in our country, and along with so
many others who sprang into action to help in whatever
way they knew how, I reached out to a former colleague
who was the head of Flight Services for American Airlines
at JFK Airport. Within the week, I was sitting down with

management and crew members teaching them breathing techniques and leading meditations in order to give them relief from the extreme anxiety and grief they were suffering.

A month after the 9-11 terrorist attack, the United States invaded Afghanistan, and two years later, the US invaded Iraq. Gurudev doesn't wait; he just takes responsibility for society. Along with conducting free trauma-relief workshops, both AOLF and IAHV also participated in "Back on Track America," a program designed to help small businesses to get back on their feet. When the Iraq war began, and in light of the escalating levels of depression, substance abuse, and suicide among our armed forces, Gurudev called me and another teacher in to discuss a new program for veterans and service members. He told us that this was the most important work we would ever do. The moment marked the start of a program that came to be called "Project Welcome Home Troops." Since that time, thousands of service members have found relief through our workshops, yet it's just a drop in the bucket in the face of America's current veteran suicide crisis.

Meanwhile, IAHV began conducting trauma-relief workshops and vocational training for thousands of women, who became widows in Iraq. A country torn apart by conflict, anger, and chronic stress that goes unchecked is fuel for the terrorists of tomorrow. AOLF-IAHV Youth Leadership Training camps provided a safe space for young people to release trauma, to become kids again and to channel their energy into becoming ambassadors of peace. IAHV's peacebuilding program for youth has now spread to Lebanon and Jordan and after my time in the Philippines last year, it's moving forward there as well.

It's an enormous task to foster human values throughout society. But after seeing people from every walk of life transform in a matter of days as a result of our programs, I have seen what is possible when like-minded people come together sharing skills, talents, resources, and love.

the ways of a guru
are unfathomable

Gurudev seemed to go out of his way to appoint one difficult personality after another to lead various aspects of our organization. He also had a way of choosing the most incompetent person possible to lead a project, not only to support that devotee's growth but to push everyone else's buttons as well. This enlightened management style meant that the opportunities to apply the knowledge in order to keep my smile were endless!

The day I learned that the only person who had ever tried to dissuade me from becoming a full-time teacher had become president of the Art of Living Foundation, I seriously started thinking about going elsewhere.

When we first met, he not only tried to persuade me not to join the organization full-time, he arrogantly told me that I could never become a "master teacher" like him.

Over time, we learned to appreciate one another's sense of humor and commitment to this path, but when it came to working together, we were like oil and water.

Enlightenment is a combination of dynamic activity with infinite patience. While I had plenty of dynamism, patience wasn't my strongest spiritual muscle at the time. Once, when I was knocking impatiently on Gurudev's door for a third time, with a sense of demand, he sent a message back through his doorkeeper. "Tell the president of IAHV to practice the value of patience."

As soon as he stepped into his new role, this man started creating more rules than I'd ever encountered in my corporate career. For everyone's sake, I did my best to find common ground, but after a while I realized, that it was a futile exercise. Things eventually became so acrimonious between us that Gurudev joked that he was losing half of his hair because of our new president and the other half because of me!

Navaratri is celebrated for nine days in India, in honor of Mother Divine, manifested in nine subtle forms. It's a time of inner reflection, fasting, prayer, meditation, and silence, which brings enormous relief to our existence. I'd been longing to attend *Navaratri* in Gurudev's presence at our Ashram in India for many years, so I was ecstatic when I got the news that I could meet him in Europe and travel to Bangalore for the celebration.

I found our new president's latest policy around travel unreasonable. He wanted me to inform him anytime I left the country, even on my own personal time. So, I ignored the policy and went about making my travel arrangements. As my plane took off for Europe, I sent him a message that I was on my way to India with Gurudev's blessings before turning my phone off.

By the time I landed in India, he'd sent several angry voicemails and fired me through email. No full-time teacher had ever been fired before now, and I scoffed at the message. My reasoning was that I was after all, in India, with the real leader of our global organization. The next day, he sent another email threatening to end my small stipend in a few weeks and informing me that I could reapply for my job in the new year.

That afternoon, I met up with Gurudev while he was feeding bananas to his pet elephant, Maheshwara. "Gurudev, I have good news and bad news. The bad news is that our president fired me today." He looked up from feeding the elephant, knowing there was more. "The good news is that I can reapply in January." Gurudev responded with, "What is he thinking?" and said that he'd speak to him. I left feeling triumphant that this was just a little blip and that it would be resolved easily. But a week later, I took the situation more seriously when I was reminded that my stipend was ending in another week. I was living from paycheck to paycheck on very little money and had used up all of my reserves. By this time, thousands of people from all over the world had arrived at our Ashram for *Navaratri*, and personal access to Gurudev was virtually nonexistent.

After another week, I was relieved to meet Gurudev during a *darshan* line, and he invited me to join him and a small group at the *Gurukul* (place of study for young pundits), where a 105-year-old Swami was about to teach a subtle and effective form of yoga. I relaxed into the invitation, assuming all was well with my return to the USA. But after the yoga session when he hadn't said anything, one of the Rishis motioned to me to speak up. I gave Gurudev an update on the situation and almost fainted when he said, "Patti, when I empower somebody, I do not interfere. You should follow the procedures."

This was not at all what I thought was going to happen! My friend, Rishiji, put his finger to his lips, indicating I shouldn't say another word. The car arrived at Gurudev's office and the moment he went in, I turned to my friend for guidance.

Rishiji said, "Gurudev may be using this situation to see how you will handle your mind in the face of a storm. It's his job after all to see that you become unshakeable. If you remain centered and cheerful, the storm will pass sooner rather than later. For now, do some self-reflection and observe what flavors of consciousness arise in your mind. We'll meet afterward."

Alone in my room, I observed how my breath became shaky with just the thought of the situation I was in. After some time, I settled down and my breath started flowing smoothly again. The situation had revealed a little bit of victim consciousness that I still had, which only made me weak when facing a challenge. The Divine was going to create these kinds of situations again and again, until I was free of it. My soul's purpose was to be a spiritual teacher and there was no way I was going to let anyone or anything stand in my way—including my own mind.

A few days later, I followed Gurudev to New Delhi where he was giving a series of public talks. It's extremely difficult to keep up with him in the capital of India, but I was determined to speak with him before returning to the States.

Using every connection I had to find out his schedule and location, I caught up with him at a talk he was giving to almost 20,000 people. Thanks to a sympathetic friend and a whole lot of luck, I arrived at the venue early and was seated in the front row. Gurudev saw me and smiled, but the moment his talk and meditation finished, it was impossible to reach him. In a flash, hundreds of people had surrounded his car, making it dangerous for even the driver to get away safely.

My plane was taking off in exactly twelve hours and panic was starting to set in. After a few rapid phone calls, I got the address where Gurudev had gone after the talk. My friend left and ten minutes later I was standing alone in front of a large apartment building in a foreign city, wondering what to do next. Saying a prayer for protection, I walked toward the security guards. The next twenty minutes was like something out of the spiritual version of a James Bond movie.

Several tall men with faces that clearly said, "Don't even think about getting past us," along with two armed security guards, watched me walk up the long driveway. The area was quiet, which was odd since there are usually hundreds of people doing their best to get even a glimpse of Gurudev when he is at a private residence. I wasn't at all sure how to proceed when a friend from the USA walked up. Together, we devised a plan to distract the guards by throwing something near the opposite gate. Our intention was to run past them and up the stairs before they knew we were gone. The plan worked, and a minute later, we were walking up endless flights of stairs looking for any sign of our Guru.

When we saw about 100 pairs of shoes outside of a door, we knew we'd come to the right place. Taking a deep breath in, I opened the door. For a moment, I just took the scene in, my breath suspended as I tried to piece together where we'd landed.

People were milling around in what appeared to be a Beauty Salon, where Gurudev had gone to bless a devotee's new business. In the next instant, there he was, rounding a corner and taking a seat in the center of the room. Before anyone knew I'd crashed their party, I slid myself onto the floor beside him. I was flustered, still catching my breath after running up all those stairs, but Gurudev acted as though nothing unusual was going on. He chatted easily with the devotees, and a few minutes later, when my friend motioned to me that it was time to go, I pleaded my case.

"Gurudev, are you really sending me back to the wolves all alone?" I asked full of uncertainty. He smiled and handed me a small statue of Krishna. "Take this back to the USA with you. I will call them when I return from Sri Lanka." He was going to Sri Lanka the next week to meet with the president of that country, in an effort to prevent civil war from breaking out. Holding tight to the little statue, I relaxed, knowing that first he would bring peace to Sri Lanka and then he would broker peace between my arch nemesis and me.

moving beyond **doubt**

Any spiritual teacher worth their salt knows that to teach knowledge, one must live it. Even if you trip 1,000 times on the path, you get up 1,000 times and keep moving forward.

A few more years passed, and once again I was traveling from New York to Washington, DC, with Gurudev during his tour. A dear friend and devotee who had built *Vishalakshi Mantap*, the new meditation hall at our Ashram in India, had recently passed away. The conversation in the car turned to the subject of death and someone asked Gurudev what happens to a yogi when they die.

"A devotee and a yogi, his *prana* will not go from the base of the spine. It will go from the higher realms. The more you purify your energy channels in the body through the strength of yoga, the more you can attain higher realms. If the mind is stable, focused at one point, at the time when the *prana* is leaving the body, then the soul gets strength to attain the highest realm." The knowledge left us silent for a while. "Gurudev, will we all go to the same Loka (a dimension in the universe) with you when we die?" I asked. "Yes! You see?" he said to my friends in the car, "there's no getting away from Patti and company!"

By "company," he was referring to a woman in the car with us, who was, to say the least, odd. Gurudev makes room for everyone on the path, and since she was devoted and adept at teaching small children, he had allowed her to become a teacher. The problem for me was that since we were both single, we were constantly roomed together during courses.

Unsure of how I would be able to afford the luxury hotel room where everyone was staying, I was both grateful and annoyed when I found out arrangements had been made for us to share a room. She was in her mid-forties with grown children, yet at 2:00 a.m. she was still bouncing on the bed and talking nonsense. Exceptionally feverish to be with Gurudev every second, she stalked me regularly thinking that I had some "special Guru Radar," that would lead her to him.

By the time I came on this trip, I was already frustrated from living on a shoestring budget and dealing with internal politics while facing the challenges that come with sharing the highest knowledge in a modern society. Just a few nights earlier, when another teacher and I were left standing in the pouring rain and refused entrance to the home where Gurudev was staying, my frustration rose even more. Adding to this was the fact that I hadn't slept well for several nights, because of my unbalanced roommate jumping on the bed at all hours of the night. While I never questioned the teachings or the teacher, I was having serious doubts about my ability to walk this path as a way of life. Everybody and everything was setting me off in one way or the other.

Gurudev had spoken to me in the past about my need for perfection. He'd encouraged me to just relax and be free, knowing that the Divine was at work in everything that was happening and only the best would happen. On one hand, I knew it was true, but still I doubted. The next morning, I was in a foul mood and just wanted to be alone. Doing my best to slip out to the airport unseen, I tiptoed past Gurudev's suite, but there is no hiding from him. As I passed by, he called out my name and I had no choice but to enter a room packed with people, wall to wall.

"Look at Patti, giving me the look she gives all her students!" he remarked. "Ooooo, isn't she scary?" he continued, egging the crowd on.

"Gurudev, are you afraid of Patti?" someone teased.

He pretended he was shaking and said, "Scared? I'm terrified!" as the room exploded in laughter. "Be careful, Patti," he added, "Your roommate has had a lot of sugar today!" Angry and humiliated, I turned and left for the airport.

It requires a lot of courage to face what is small in ourselves, in order to be free of it. And a Guru, who knows his student's consciousness, will skillfully turn the heat up and down, depending on the need.

Hurrying to board the flight before Gurudev arrived, I dropped my luggage off and proceeded toward the gate. But, just as I turned the corner, there he was, standing with a group of devotees and looking straight at me.

By now my head was throbbing from all the emotion I'd bottled up over the past few months. The second I walked up to him, the teasing started all over again. Doing my best to refrain from showing even a hint of emotion on my face, eventually he said something so funny I had to grit my teeth to keep from laughing.

"Patti is trying so hard to be tough, but her smile is starting to come through!" he said, pointing at me. I could feel the walls of my ego starting to come down just a little... but still, I wasn't giving in. When he kept making jokes, saying that his hair had become gray and he was losing more of it, because I was on the same trip with him, the wall quickly went back up.

Normally, Gurudev and I enjoy a good repartee, but right now I was way off my center and getting disturbed by anything and everything. After some time, I just stood off to the side by myself. That's when Gurudev came up to me.

"You're really grumpy today. Tell me, what is it?"

And with that, the entire façade I'd put up to pretend I was dealing well with the transition from my old life to this new life came crashing down. I was flying by the seat of my pants on just about everything, with no playbook. Complaint after complaint spilled out while Gurudev patiently listened. "I just don't know if I want to do this anymore, Gurudev. I don't know if I'm cut out for this life."

The next thing I knew the gate agent made the last call to board, and I had to hurry down the jet bridge. Gurudev was already in his seat as I passed, and pointed to the seat next to him. "Patti, sit here."

"I can't, Gurudev. I'm in another seat."

He repeated, "Patti, sit here."

"Gurudev, it's another devotee's seat, and she will be mad at me."

"Patti, sit here, now. Give her your seat."

I sat down while he allowed me to continue rattling on with a long list of complaints. From all I've seen through my many years with Gurudev, his level of patience and compassion is unparalleled. After a while, when I was just repeating myself, he snapped his fingers and said, "Present moment, Patti! Present moment!"

It was amazing. In that very moment, awareness kicked in, and all the complaints and doubts left. And just like that, I was back to myself, humorously sharing anecdotes about the things I'd experienced around this odd woman over the last few days. The more stories I shared, the harder Gurudev laughed. "Two hours with you on this flight? I'm laughing too hard!" he said while holding his stomach from laughter while the plane continued boarding.

Joy is found in the present moment.

A complaining mind usually complains about things that happened in the past. When we do not look forward to the future with a positive mindset, and when our *prana* (life force energy) is low, then our mind tends to get entangled with the events of the past, and it starts to regret or complain about them. Just smile and move forward. Your complaining does not help improve or resolve anything. So forget about the past and stop worrying about the future. Once you have faith about your future, then you don't worry about it. Joy is rejoicing in what is and sorrow is craving for what isn't.

—Sri Sri Ravi Shankar

And as if on cue, there she was—the same woman—now boarding at the front of the airplane. Clutching a sack full of papers, with her glasses sitting crooked on her nose, she looked like a cartoon character of an absent-minded professor. Before I knew what was happening, in a voice loud enough for everyone to hear, she exclaimed, "Well Montella—you've got the Guru now and you've got me—what else do you want?"

I held my breath in anticipation of what else she might say. Standing in the aisle, while all the passengers behind her had to wait, she took her time adjusting her glasses and shuffling more books and papers back and forth while glaring at me, before proceeding to her seat. Once she passed, I let out a big sigh of relief and Gurudev started laughing all over again.

hurricane **katrina**

In 2005, along with the rest of America, I watched the news in disbelief as Hurricane Katrina flooded the city of New Orleans after the levees broke. Horrific scene after scene of people being lashed by the rain on their rooftops and desperate for help flashed across the television screen while reporters cried out to the government to respond. In a last-ditch effort for shelter, thousands of people evacuated to the Superdome convention center, in spite of there being no provisions for food, water, or medical attention. The next day, on the news, I saw a mother crying and begging for water, while holding her baby who was dying of dehydration. Some of the elderly died in their wheelchairs and were left on streets or in corners of the Superdome, with nothing more than a towel covering their face and a piece of paper listing their name and next of kin.

By now, I'd been teaching in New Orleans for a few years and immediately started calling our volunteers and teachers to see if they were safe and how I could help. Within days of the disaster, one of our devotees, who was also a doctor, called me seeking guidance. She had evacuated to Baton Rouge and was working in a makeshift triage unit on the university lawn. She said that the doctors were seeing untold misery and they were absolutely exhausted from dealing with their own personal trauma while also caring for patient after patient. They didn't have enough help or medical resources for the humungous task at hand and she wanted to know what could be done in between shifts to help her colleagues.

After two days, with still no sign of government intervention, I called Gurudev in Rishikesh to ask for help. He immediately offered to fly to America, but all the roads and airports were closed into and out of New Orleans and Baton Rouge, as the flooding and disaster relief continued. Evacuees were on their way to temporary shelters throughout Texas. After receiving guidance on how to address the trauma, I promised to keep him apprised of the developing situation and set about helping to organize AOLF-IAHV's first disaster relief effort in America. I wrote down the wisdom he shared in anticipation of what was to come: *"We value life more than anything else. Hold onto these values. How many of us would like to keep our smile in the toughest time? To smile is not a big deal—anyone can do it. It means something to smile when everything has gone haywire. Live in the Present Moment means this moment—let's be* alive! *This is our moment."*

The next day, several enthusiastic college students and another teacher from Canada joined our volunteer efforts. No one was really prepared for the extraordinary humanitarian crisis including our government leaders, and yet, it seemed that almost everyone who could rose to the challenge with open minds and hearts.

The first few days we just kept showing up at the Austin convention center, determined to be of service to the evacuees and anyone else we could help. Traumatized people of every age—some older than 100 and newborn babies—arrived frightened, hungry, and dehydrated. The convention center was organized chaos, and by day two, many nonprofits and religious groups were refused entry. But we kept showing up and on day three, armed with bottles of water and determination, we partnered with the Global Brotherhood of Light Youth Ministries and started serving the evacuees inside the convention center.

We walked the halls of the convention center day and night, offering guided meditations to anyone who wanted relief including first responders and other nonprofits. While people wanted peace of mind—in fact, they were desperate for it—most were too tired or overwhelmed to even walk up the stairs or down the hall to where we were teaching. We did what was needed in each moment; sometimes it was giving comfort by holding a hand and listening to someone's story, other times it was playing a game with the children, and sometimes we led a meditation.

After an evacuee and their family had cots to sleep on, they went about finding temporary housing and work while searching for family and friends lost in the hurricane. With all that was going on, it didn't take long to notice that the kids were getting lost in the shuffle and were in dire need of attention.

But finding a suitable space in the convention center to lead breathing techniques and meditations was another matter altogether. The decision-makers changed hands and policies daily, making every day an uphill battle while the operation sorted itself out.

I shared the challenges we were facing with a former student, who was a civic leader. He worked closely with the local police and graciously arranged for me to attend one of the mayor's press conferences. His friends on the force were very kind and showed me where to stand so that I could meet the mayor the moment he left the room. Our chapter had earned a good reputation and I'd met Mayor Wynn previously, through a grant the city council had awarded our foundation. I hoped he would remember my name and face. The precise moment the mayor left the conference, I was on his heels explaining our plight at the convention center. The squeaky wheel got the grease, and I'm forever grateful to him for arranging a room we could teach in on the spot.

Our first program for youth started a few days later. My heart melted when one young man commented, "The breathing techniques brought me so much peace of mind, I even forgot about the hurricane."

One evening—away from any media glare—a few of us attended a dinner and live music event organized for the evacuees by a famous movie star from Austin. The sound of the vibrant zydeco music brought everyone to the dance floor, including me. After a few dances, I noticed a few older people still sitting and went over to encourage them to join us.

"Oh honey, I would if I could," said one woman. "But my legs are still swollen from standing in the water for so long during the hurricane, just waiting for help." I stayed with her and her friends for the rest of the evening and held her hand as we swayed to the music.

Over the weeks that followed, more and more people left the convention center to move in with family or into temporary housing provided by the city. Eventually, we moved our programs over to as many housing complexes that would have us, which again was not an easy situation to organize, but we were able to get the job done.

Gurudev planned to visit the region to meet with evacuees and volunteers and, in collaboration with the mayor's office, we began making arrangements for his arrival. After meeting with Mayor Wynn, Gurudev was also scheduled to speak at a housing complex where we'd been teaching. It was extremely hot and humid that day— over 100 degrees. Yet in spite of the weather, the tent was full of people eager to meet Gurudev and receive his blessings. Just as we were about to leave for another meeting, I was asked to delay Gurudev's departure. An elderly man of more than 100 years wanted to meet Gurudev; he was in a wheelchair and unable to meet him in the main tent. A few minutes later, dressed in his Sunday best and smiling from ear to ear, the elderly man rolled himself out of the rundown housing complex and toward Gurudev. I thought my heart would burst with love as Gurudev bent down to speak with him and the man closed his eyes in prayer, to receive a blessing. We were just about to drive away a second time, when a boy not more than ten years old knocked on Gurudev's window. He wanted to show Gurudev a sketch he'd done of him. Gurudev praised the young man, and full of pride, the boy placed it in his hands.

Months later, I returned to New Orleans. The usual policy of staying with a devotee wasn't possible, as most homes were under construction or demolished since most of the city had been flooded. I ended up staying in a toxic-smelling government trailer that my student wasn't using. She opted to stay in her home, in spite of the mold and the massive construction it was under.

Like many people from the area, she was used to hurricanes and had chosen to stay in her home to care for a pregnant neighbor. When the reports started coming in about the strength of the hurricane, her husband begged her to evacuate to Houston with him, but she remained where she was unaware of the historical disaster that was about to unfold. When she woke the next morning to no electricity, water gushing from the ceiling, felled trees and the outdoor furniture in the pool, she had no idea what had taken place. She said, "I walked outside and it looked like the world had ended. Trees were uprooted, the streets were flooded. It was eerie. There wasn't a sound or a person around. It felt apocalyptic." Finally, a neighbor came out and filled her in on the death and devastation across the city. She couldn't make it to be with her pregnant friend and prayed that she and her young son were ok on the top level of their condominium. Frightened and alone, she didn't know what to do or where to go. There was no food, no electricity, no water, and no help. Pulling a lawn chair out of the pool, she sat down to do the *Sudarshan Kriya*. She said, "I told myself that if this was as powerful as I thought it was, then now was the time." Afterward, she felt calm and clear enough to pack up a few things and started walking toward the convention center with her dog. Luckily, by the time she arrived, there was one seat left, on a bus headed to Houston, where she was able to join her husband.

That week, I taught a program at Ochsner Hospital, which was able to remain open during the hurricane. A physician who practiced the *Sudarshan Kriya* had arranged a course for a group of doctors and emergency room nurses. These caretakers had been there for thousands of people physically impacted by Hurricane Katrina, often in the dark, by generator, and in the midst of untold chaos and fear. At the same time that they were helping so many others, their own homes and families were severely impacted by the floods, just like the people they were serving.

The stress and pressure of what the medical community had been through had taken its toll on far too many in their field. They told me that suicide, substance abuse, infidelity, and broken relationships had become a regular part of daily life either for them or their loved ones.

A cardiac nurse, who had learned our breathing practices a few months earlier, was repeating the program with me. In addition to losing her home and possessions during the disaster, her mother had passed three months later. She shared that when she returned to the home she had lived in for twenty-five years, she realized that what was important were the memories, not the house itself. What had been a place of safety was now more like a jungle with overgrown vegetation everywhere. There was a terrible stench in the house, nauseating in fact, due to the rotted vegetation and overwhelming heat. She and her husband started cleaning things up without any help and it wasn't until spring that they even had electricity or city services of any kind—a full nine months after the hurricane. She shared that the first AOLF course had helped her to let go of a lot, but since repeating the course, the knowledge had sunk in to an even deeper level. Now, she was able to accept what had happened, without such a strong emotional reaction. She was living more in the present moment instead of being an emotional see-saw. "People would tell me that I was holding up so well. The truth was, I was just holding it all in and walling myself off from people, internalizing everything that had happened. After practicing the *Sudarshan Kriya* I was able to purge the grief, along with my attachment to all of our possessions. Before this, I had material wealth; now I have spiritual wealth. I've learned to focus more on what's of value like family and friends," she said. "Now, I'm more connected with life."

Our foundation eventually opened a center in New Orleans and serves the community to this day.

one world **family**

I was back in India to celebrate Gurudev's vision of *Vasudhaiva Kutumbakam* (One World Family) during our foundation's twenty-five-year Silver Jubilee Anniversary that coincided with his fiftieth birthday. The three-day event united more than three million people from 150 countries, including more than 1,000 leaders representing ten major world religions and 750 political figures. In spite of Gurudev receiving numerous death threats, this first-of-its-kind extravaganza unfolded peacefully as millions gathered in Bangalore and across the world to embrace non-violence, universal love and human values. A hilarious and educational book about what took place behind the scenes to orchestrate such a massive global event could easily become a best-seller!

To begin with, finding a venue to accommodate millions of people was in and of itself a challenge. Jakkur Airfield served our purpose, but first it had to be made free of bacteria and mosquitos. This effort required acquiring huge amounts of cow dung, well-known in India as an inexpensive cleansing agent and mosquito repellent. In fact, cow dung was a topic spoken about so often during our organizing meetings that we joked that our volunteers were carrying buckets to capture the substance as it spontaneously became available throughout the day! The 3.5-acre airfield also had a snake situation, which resulted in the hiring of snake charmers to safely catch and transfer the reptiles to another location.

The launch of the year-long worldwide celebrations was a thrilling experience from the moment I put my suitcases down in the enormous reception tent at our Ashram in India.

People from all around the world arrived by the busload day and night. Adding to the intense amount of activity taking place throughout the day was the constant stream of official government cars carrying politicians and dignitaries along with an influx of Swamis, Sadhus, Priests, Nuns, and Saints from all traditions. Every morning, over a cup of chai at the café, I'd watch the day unfold, as though it was a television documentary on how many different kinds of people can fit into one Ashram. Gurudev always says that the whole world is our family; it looked as though they were all showing up at one place.

At the time, Bangalore was a city of around one million people and roads had to be built to accommodate the enormous number of guests arriving for the celebration. Accommodations for so many people required some very creative planning. Business owners donated empty office space, schools opened up their facilities, and hundreds of volunteers hosted as many guests as they could. We assumed that there would be major traffic jams the day of the event, with millions of people traveling to one venue, yet everyone arrived safely, in no time at all.

I stood proudly along with millions of others as Gurudev's vision came to light during the ceremonial lighting of the lamp, inaugurating the Silver Jubilee celebrations. Sri A.P.J. Abdul Kalam, then president of India, remarked, "If you can have a mind of a scientist and the spiritual force that His Holiness Sri Sri Ravi Shankar gives, then we can have a beautiful world, a happy world, a prosperous world."

The stage, engineered in the Hampi architecture of Karnataka India, was Gurudev's vision. The size of four football fields, it was built to accommodate about 5,000 people along with a symphony of nearly 4,000 musicians from South India. Security was understandably tight with so many dignitaries in attendance, so for safety reasons, seating on stage was restricted. Even Gurudev's own father was turned away by mistake the first evening by over-zealous security guards! My friend Susannah, who had temporarily lost some of her sight, was one of the musicians and as her helper, I was able to sit on stage.

The three-day extravaganza continued without incident, until the last evening when the stage started shaking from the weight of more people than it was built to accommodate.

It is customary in the Vedic tradition to construct statues in honor of the deva (angel) energy. One of these figures, which contained a powerful energy, was present on stage for the final celebration. When Gurudev saw the men responsible for carrying the platform that holds the elaborately decorated deity leave the stage because it was shaking, he knew something was amiss. Word immediately came down that all the teachers had to immediately leave the stage, and all was well.

Just as we were walking out, disappointment turned to excitement when Gurudev invited us to meet him at the home of a devotee after the event. Walking up to a large home magnificently decorated with flowers and lights of every color to welcome Gurudev and hundreds of his guests, I couldn't have felt happier. It was a warm and intimate closing to a massive global experience, with Gurudev and friends, old and new, from around the world.

The next day was Monday, which is the day Gurudev performs the *Rudram*, a sacred chant in honor of Shiva, and I'd heard that he might lead it at the airfield. With only a few hours of sleep, I crossed my fingers that my intuition was right. Most of my friends had planned to return to the Ashram in the afternoon, while Susannah and I caught a taxi to the airfield just as the sun was rising.

The sight of the now empty airfield, which had been bustling with millions of diverse people less than eight hours earlier, was astonishing. The grounds and air, so colorful with costumes and people the night before, now melded together in one bland color of beige. The TV cameras and symphony were all gone, and the only sound was a single piece of loose paper riding the currents of the wind. Any hint of the massive gathering from the days before was nonexistent.

Unsure of where the ceremony would take place, if indeed Gurudev had gotten there at 7:00 a.m., we walked toward the stage, which was almost entirely disassembled except for one main platform. And to our delight, there stood Gurudev—alone, in a simple white cotton *dhoti*, his garments gently waving in the breeze. He was single-handedly orchestrating seating arrangements for all the farmers and villagers who had gathered. I just stood there for a moment, taking in the scene.

Gurudev is referred to as a Guru of the people, and this morning was a beautiful testament of that truth. Susannah and I jumped on stage to help him with the seating arrangements. Once everything was ready, Gurudev led the ancient chant, while we did our best to encourage people to stay in rhythm. The simplicity and purity of the morning remains one of my favorite memories with Gurudev.

A few days later, a group of us headed to Delhi to celebrate *Shivaratri* with Gurudev, when I became very ill. Although

I wasn't able to attend the events that evening, I took refuge in the sound of the local temple bells and chants to Shiva, just outside my bedroom window. I was well enough to travel to Rishikesh the next day, with Gurudev and the other "old-timers" on the path, to attend our first Blessings Course on the banks of the sacred Ganges River.

To me, enjoying the ancient city of Rishikesh with Gurudev is one of the best ways to spend time on this planet. It was my second trip to the holy city, and this time I was a lot more at ease with the culture. I knew where to enjoy a local tea and toast, and the Ashram where we stayed was familiar. It was heaven on earth to wake up and see the Ganges River out of one window and the Himalayan Mountains out of the other. My only disappointment was that Gurudev was staying on the other side of the river, about a thirty-minute walk across a very long suspension bridge.

Every evening after class, I jumped onto a scooter to attend *satsang* on the other side of the river with Gurudev, in spite of the fact that it was in Hindi. I'd never seen men and women separated during *satsang* before and was surprised to learn that this was the custom in Rishikesh. Sitting down next to smiling aunties from the village, I was happy to be there whether or not I understood a word. Usually, Gurudev is escorted out of the area before a throng of people engulfs him, and yet, somehow I was fortunate enough to catch his eye just before he left. He asked me how the course was going and how people were enjoying it, but before I could answer, the security detail and the crowd pulled him away, which meant it was time for me to cross the bridge again—just in time for lights out.

The meditations led by one of our Swamis were out of this world. The last day of the program was a life-changing moment for me, when the *siddhi* (Divine power) to bless is invoked through the grace of the Guru. Afterward, I walked alone in silence toward the sacred Ganges River, in the same sand that millions of Saints and Sadhus have walked on for millennia before me. I couldn't help but contemplate death as I passed skulls of monkeys on my way to sit on a large rock in the river. Sitting there, with the waves lapping at my feet, I felt as though a part of me had died in this process. So many impressions that had fueled negative emotions of doubt, disappointment, frustration, and disillusionment were now gone.

The feeling was one of total purity, freedom, and unconditional love. I became acutely aware of one energy moving through the universe that connects us all. The knowledge I'd been taught and had struggled to grasp—that there is no "other"—made more sense to me than ever before.

The minute class was over I ran across the bridge to meet with Gurudev. Knocking on his door, I felt a tap on my shoulder and turned around to see my friends, Michael, Jeff, and John right behind me. We met Gurudev on the top floor of the *kutir* where he was sitting on a traditional Indian swing, on the patio. He seemed happy to see us. "Look at your eyes! You're all so bright I have to put sunglasses on!" he exclaimed, as we beamed back with joy and gratitude for all we'd received.

The next afternoon, I was on a ghat (boat) with Gurudev and some others, crossing the Ganges just after everyone had taken a dip in the river. Our clothes were dripping wet but our eyes were glistening with happiness! Someone who I was jealous of at the time was also on the boat. Gurudev mentioned to him how bright I was after taking the course and as I was basking in the praise, the next thing I knew, he was praising this person to the high heavens. Taking it in stride, I kept quiet.

Once the ghat landed at the dock, a huge crowd ran after Gurudev. I tried to get past the crowd by climbing over a railing connected to some concrete stairs, which turned out to be a bad idea. Someone pulled on my bag in an attempt to climb over me so that he could get closer to Gurudev. He pulled on my bag so hard, that I fell several feet. I landed on hard sand and the wind was knocked out of me. Meanwhile, the crowd just kept moving; no one even saw what had happened. Wet from the river and winded from the fall, I started going into shock; thankfully, the grace kicked in at that precise moment.

Someone whistled to a devotee on a scooter and together they helped me to climb on the back of it. The driver was directed to take me straight to one of our Swamis at the Ashram. Swamiji and his wife lovingly took care of me, giving me some herbs for any internal bruising along with hot milk and turmeric to address any possible infection and to help my nervous system to settle down. They dried my clothes and hair, and once I was done I went to *satsang*. By the next morning, I was in a lot of pain from back spasms. Gritting my teeth from the pain, I knocked on Gurudev's door.

He started teasing me again about being an old woman. "Well, I really do feel like an old woman today," I said, and shared what had happened. Gurudev called me forward for *prasad* (blessed food) and told me to eat it immediately. Miraculously, by the time I walked out the door ten minutes later, every bit of pain in my back had disappeared and I was standing up straight again.

the power of **prayer**

The next year, I was on a small airplane with Gurudev and about fifteen devotees on our way to the Canadian Ashram, when he gave me a lesson, a scolding, and a blessing all rolled into one!

I was thrilled to learn that I was sitting next to Gurudev on the flight, but when I got there, someone else was already in my seat and in deep conversation with him. He assured me that I'd be called back after the flight took off, so I found another seat. A little while later, Gurudev called for me and while I was buckling my seat belt, he made a powerful statement. He said, "You're not using your power of prayer or your power to bless."

I knew that I was simply an instrument for the Divine, yet I felt shy about blessing people in spite of seeing how it could help. The first time I blessed someone was when we were driving back from one part of Colorado to another very late at night, through a snowy and dangerous mountain pass. The driver was suffering from a dry eye condition and couldn't continue driving. Immediately after a blessing, his eye condition cleared up and we safely made it back home.

Without another word, Gurudev called someone else up to take my seat. I took some time to reflect on his words before deciding to have a little fun of my own, rather than being frustrated by this game of musical chairs. Standing in the small aisle of the plane, I held my boarding pass out for the flight attendant, who had been watching all of us. "Don't you think I should be allowed to sit in my own assigned seat?" I asked her.

"I'm not getting into this!" she laughed and kept moving.

It was clear that if I wanted to continue sitting next to Gurudev, I had to take things into my own hands. Next, I did my best to engage the other passengers near us, to support me. "Can I get a show of hands of the people who agree that I should sit in my assigned seat?" There were some snickers and laughter, and when one man raised his hand I encouraged others to follow his lead, but no one else was willing. Gurudev watched the play from his seat, where yet another person was now sitting. When the plane suddenly took a dip indicating we were about to land, I seized the opportunity and with a sense of urgency in my voice, I said, "Hurry! Get up and go back to your seat. The plane is landing!" It did the trick and I slid back into my seat, triumphantly, smiling at Gurudev.

purified in the fire
of criticism

Our Silver Jubilee celebrations continued around the globe for another year, ending in Washington, DC, with an event at the prestigious Kennedy Center. At the time, I was the national director of media and along with that responsibility and a few others, I was asked to temporarily move to DC.

We had just purchased a new center that was currently under heavy construction. I moved into a small bedroom on the top floor, which meant that every day I woke up coughing from dust and covering my ears from the steady sound of hammers, saws, and drills.

Through a mutual friend, I was introduced to Rene, an assistant professor of military and emergency medicine at the Uniformed Services University of the Health Sciences.

Along with her impressive credentials, Rene was warm-hearted and interested in holistic approaches to help veterans recover from the trauma of war. We became instant friends. Together, we organized a course for combat veterans, military researchers, and medical staff.

Meanwhile, I formed a volunteer media team of excellent speakers, writers, and thinkers, but none of them were journalists. Days and evenings became a blur of strategizing, planning, teaching, and endless meetings as we prepared for an event in a few months that typically requires a year of planning.

The White House Correspondents' dinner was taking place the night of our event, and every major news agency in town planned to attend it. This took the challenge of getting media coverage for our event to a whole new level. Nonetheless, we pressed on, even wrapping our press packets in bright red paper and personally delivering them to media mailrooms, just to stand out amongst hundreds of others.

I was pleased when two international media houses confirmed interviews with Gurudev and a national news outlet agreed to cover our pre-event. Everything seemed to be working out on my end—until it wasn't. The day Gurudev arrived in DC, one of the news outlets canceled, the other was a no-show, and the third canceled thirty minutes before the event. I was confused, embarrassed, and heartbroken.

Regardless, the Silver Jubilee event was a huge success. It was an illustrious gathering of scientists, educators, prominent members of Congress, including then-Senator Joseph Biden, and high-ranking United Nations representatives. People from every segment of society—heads of Veterans organizations as well as high school students and former gang members—shared powerful stories of transformation and their appreciation for Gurudev and the Art of Living Foundation. Afterward, I hurriedly prepared a press release for our media office in India who was anxiously waiting.

Our ability to accept and self-reflect when criticised indicates how much we have grown.

Every time you face criticism, know that you are vast like the ocean and you can take in anything. Otherwise, we get off balance. When you feel small, that is when you don't feel like taking criticism. When you feel very big, then you think, "I am much bigger than this criticism, let me take it in."

—Sri Sri Ravi Shankar

After a long day, when everything was finally done, I joined my peers who were celebrating in Gurudev's suite. Gurudev was handing out silver medallions to all the volunteers in recognition of their service, and the room was filled with a mixture of joy and relief, after an entire year of twenty-fifth-anniversary celebrations!

"The entire event was a huge success!" Gurudev declared, while everyone nodded in agreement and cheered. "Except media," he said. "Media was a complete failure."

You could have heard a pin drop.

A few of my colleagues came to the defense of the media team, pointing out how dedicated our team was, and how hard we'd worked. Gurudev wasn't having any of it. "Media was a complete failure," he reiterated.

I knew by now that defense consciousness would only make me look smaller than I was already feeling. At the same time, my intuition told me that this wasn't really about media—something else was at play. I kept quiet while others chimed in, pointing out how difficult it had been to get media coverage in a large city like DC, especially without a professional public relations firm along with a lot of other reasons.

The discussion continued and at one point, Gurudev caught my eye. I silently indicated that I was ready to take even more criticism. He smiled at me and in an instant I felt as though I'd been filled with liquid love...just before he turned up the heat.

By now, even more people had entered the room, and had joined in the discussion, as though I wasn't even in the room! At one point, the intensity of the situation became too much. As soon as Gurudev stood up to leave, I slid out the door as quickly as possible. It had been a long three months and an even longer day, and I was exhausted. Hiding out in my hotel room, I cried and cried, releasing months of stress, self-doubt, and disappointment.

Gurudev was leaving for the airport early the next morning, and while I would normally join everyone to see him off, I stayed back. After some time, his nephew called looking for me. Full of false pride, I retorted, "I'm unavailable," and said goodbye. Several more attempts were made to get me to the airport by different people and by the third call, I stopped picking up the phone. Once I returned home to Colorado, I moved on and got back to work. Later that year, with the experience behind me, I asked Gurudev what I could have done better. "We go from failure to success. Live in the present moment," was all he said.

That summer, I took some time off to spend time with Gurudev at our Canadian Ashram. I soaked up the silence of long walks in the woods, afternoons at the lake, restful meditations and *satsangs* rich with knowledge. I was relaxing on my version of a summer holiday, when it all came to a screeching halt. I was scheduled to travel with Gurudev to California for our annual Guru Purnima celebrations the following week. That morning, Gurudev received a call requesting me to come early to California to work on media. "Vacation is over!" he said, after giving me the news. I wanted to throw up.

How was it possible that nature had put me right back into the exact same situation I'd just gone through? Once again, not only did we not have much media coverage in

California, no one had done any outreach and the event was taking place in a week. I had no idea where I was going to stay, who was picking me up or how I would get around Los Angeles. "Everything will work out once you land," Gurudev reassured me. A few hours later, on a wing and a prayer, I boarded a flight to Los Angeles and true to his word, by the time I landed everything was in place.

A cheerful psychologist and fellow Art of Living teacher met me at the airport. She had graciously adjusted her schedule and set up a room for me in her home until it was time to go to Pomona for Guru Purnima. Over dinner, I laid out my dilemma and she mentioned that she happened to know the diner where a famous television news host ate breakfast every morning; she just didn't know what time he would be there.

Our organization's humanitarian efforts, led by Gurudev, were providing holistic trauma relief for people who were suffering from war, in a way that was making a big difference. I was committed to sharing what we had to offer to the world one way or the other. So the next morning by 7:00 a.m. I was at the diner, press kit in hand and a fierce determination in my heart. I shared my plight with a sympathetic waitress who seated me across from the television celebrity's usual booth.

An hour later, the television news host was sitting across the aisle from me, having breakfast with his old cronies, all of them accomplished TV and film personalities. I started making friendly conversation before boldly pressing a media kit into his hands and earnestly telling him all about the work of Sri Sri Ravi Shankar and the Art of Living Foundation.

Gurudev's recent tour to Iraq, as the first Hindu spiritual leader to be invited by the government, was unprecedented. During his visit he had opened up a productive dialogue among inter-religious leaders about how to bring forth human values as one nation. Before he left, the Islamic government had also agreed to send a group of youth delegates to attend our Leadership Development training in India. During this time, the number of widows in Iraq was rising dramatically. While other NGOs were temporarily leaving the conflict areas, IAHV's teachers and volunteers were actively conducting vocational training programs for the widows and organizing Ayurvedic health camps, while also leading trauma relief workshops.

As he was giving me the number of his assistant who would see about an interview, my phone rang. To my amazement, another prominent news anchor was on the other line requesting an interview with Gurudev. Excitedly, I called Gurudev's office to schedule this "sure thing," but elation quickly turned to deflation when I was told that his LA schedule was packed and that an in-person interview with CNN wouldn't be possible. I hung up, steadied my mind, and set forth an intention that come what may, this interview was going to happen.

Over the next few days, I tap danced between CNN and Gurudev's schedulers, while coordinating the delivery of film from his tour of Iraq. CNN called me daily to check on the status of the interview, while Gurudev's office simultaneously held me at bay. Nonetheless, I remained steadfast. Finally, I got the green light to proceed, dialed CNN, and moved forward with the rest of the arrangements.

The day of the interview, I drove to Los Angeles with Gurudev for what turned out to be our first national news interview in the USA. Once we left the building, Gurudev turned to me and said, simply, "Success."

There's a saying in India that the more you rub a piece of sandalwood, the more fragrance comes out of it; the more you hit gold, the more it shines; and the more you crush sugarcane the more it gives of its sweet juices.

The wisdom of the Vedas is to be unattached to the fruits of our actions and to serve just for the sake of serving. Getting caught up in thinking that I was in control of things and becoming feverish for a positive outcome had actually led to failure. Once I became centered and just did my job without worrying about the outcome, things unfolded almost effortlessly. With just a little shift of consciousness, my work went from being a problem to an adventure.

things just got
a little weirder

Gurudev leads with a light touch—just enough to hold the picture in the frame. It's both empowering and challenging, especially for someone coming from the structured corporate world. By the time he arrived in Houston during one of his USA tours, I had reached the end of my rope from dealing with so many issues and difficult people.

I was embarrassed to have to speak to him about small issues, preferring to find solutions myself; however, I just kept hitting wall after wall. As always, he took the news in stride, assuring me that everyone would be happy and things would smooth out. "We're a heterogeneous organization," he said. The skill is to learn how to work with all types of personalities and challenging situations in order to get the job done with a peaceful mind." It sounded noble, but I seriously wondered if it was possible.

Leave a little room for imperfection.

Imperfections exist at three levels: physical, mental, and emotional, i.e., body, thought, and emotions. If you don't accept the imperfections on the physical level, you become more and more imperfect on the mental and emotional level. This acceptance, of a little bit of imperfection on the periphery, allows you to be more patient and calm and ensures that you at least maintain the inner perfection.

—Sri Sri Ravi Shankar

By the time I met him the next day, I was in a pretty sour mood. "Oh Patti, you are so inspiring!" he remarked. "Especially when you're silent!" Both my smile and my sense of humor had "taken a toss," as Gurudev would say, and I left to put out more fires.

That night, my old pattern of taking off when a situation becomes intolerable was back in full swing. Sensing something was up, my dear friend Caroline knocked on my door, just as I was about to purchase a bus ticket back to Austin.

"You can certainly leave, that's no problem. But you chose to follow a true Guru on a spiritual path and he's leading you to enlightenment. If you leave now, and you don't apply the knowledge to get through what's bothering you, there will be a karmic tax to pay since you have the knowledge and aren't using it. Gurudev calls this, the Great Blunder."

She was right. I knew by now that a Divine power was with me, and that if I stayed the course, things would work out. Still, it requires enormous commitment and dedication to trust in something bigger than yourself. I meditated on it and by the next morning, I was back on track.

From Texas, a few of us traveled with Gurudev to the East Coast, for a teacher refresher meeting. While the people I was upset with were good at heart, I didn't approve of how they were treating our volunteers. During the flight, Gurudev took the time to broaden my perspective. "Patti, not only does our organization do much good for people worldwide, it's a vehicle for you to become rooted in the knowledge. Bliss comes out of chaos, and the ability to enjoy chaos is enlightenment." He assured me that he was aware of who was creating trouble for others and that he would take care of it, adding, "I want you to become unshakeable, come what may."

Our hosts organized a large *satsang* in their beautiful home and invited a few neighbors. People from every walk of life regularly come to meet Gurudev, from recovering addicts to titans of industry and heads of state. This time it was an alleged Mafia boss who came to meet Gurudev; all I could do was wonder. After he left, another surprise guest showed up. This man loved Gurudev. He had been on and off the path and had just lost his successful business and marriage due to substance abuse. Although he was not a teacher, he came to meet Gurudev right out of a rehabilitation facility. Each day, while we met with Gurudev in a room with large windows overlooking rolling green hills, I saw this man pacing back and forth, glued to both his phone and his cigarettes. I was even more surprised to see him on our flight the next day, sitting next to Gurudev.

We were flying to San Antonio with a connection in Dallas, before Gurudev would continue on to Germany. When we deplaned, Gurudev instructed me to stay back in Dallas until he returned for his flight to Germany. "He just got out of rehabilitation and can't be left alone," he said before adding, "I'll be back soon!" I stood there dumbfounded. Swallowing my disappointment, I turned to my charge who had a limousine waiting to take him to an Alcoholics Anonymous (AA) meeting. I had no choice but to accompany him.

I wondered how in the world I'd gone from traveling with an enlightened Master to attending an AA meeting with a virtual stranger in a matter of minutes. I had no idea how this was going to work, since AA meetings are a private and sacred space for recovering alcoholics. We walked into the meeting and when it was my turn to introduce myself, all I could say was my name and that I was *not* an alcoholic, hoping that I didn't upset anyone.

After my surprise introduction, the group took a few minutes to decide if I could stay for the meeting, and in the end agreed no harm done.

After the meeting, in spite of the fact that this man's wife had just left him and his business was spiraling downward, he wanted to visit a famous jewelry store to buy a diamond ring for his new girlfriend. I chanted mantras to myself for patience, while waiting for this absurd situation to be over. Seven hours later, I was back at the airport, waiting for Gurudev to deplane. I reserved a club room for him, since there was a two-hour layover before his flight to Germany departed. I told my recovering friend to wait there. It had been a difficult day taking care of someone who was so painfully restless and unaware, and I wanted to meet Gurudev at the gate on my own. The more bizarre things became, the more inward I had gone, in order to manage my own peace of mind and patience. As soon as Gurudev saw me, he exclaimed, "Look how bright you are! You're glowing!" and handed me a rose.

"Well, it's quite possible after what I've been through in the last seven hours that I am now enlightened!" I said.

"You're not taking my job away from me, are you?" he replied.

"Gurudev, you won't believe what it's been like or where I've been, " I answered.

He laughed and said, "Well, one thing is for sure— there's never a dull moment in the Art of Living!"

not-so-subtle **yoga**

The Divine feminine is revered in the ancient Vedic tradition. Thousands of years ago, women held some of the most powerful positions in society, ranging from education and finance to defense. Gurudev has spoken about how this dynamic began to change sometime around the Middle Ages when men became afraid that women would become too powerful, so limited women's education, preventing them from learning even the ancient Vedic chants.

In Gurudev's eyes, however, everyone is equal, and naively, I believed that everyone in our organization felt the same. In retrospect, this belief was unrealistic; the same issues around gender equality that women face in our patriarchal society were alive and well in our own small organization.

The personality clashes between me and the new president of our organization continued, and one day he went too far. But this time, rather than getting upset by his latest insulting remark, which I would have done in the past, I asked for a few weeks to consider the demeaning suggestion he'd made regarding my future with the organization. Determined to find a more skillful approach to the unpleasant dynamics once and for all, I knew it was time for bold action. So without a word to anyone, I booked a flight to Germany to coincide with Gurudev's arrival at the Ashram.

He was walking to the meditation hall when to his surprise, I called out his name. I discussed the situation I was up against in detail, along with presenting him a strategy that I believed would lead to a solution.

Gurudev was scheduled to fly to Washington, DC in a few days to meet with the president and Board, and I had booked my travel to meet up with him afterward, in Canada. But the night before our flights, he requested that I fly to Washington, DC, with him before continuing on. I really didn't want to go to DC no matter what, and did my best to get out of it—to no avail.

As I walked with Gurudev toward the arrivals area, the music from the movie "Chariots of Fire" (about two athletes who run for God and against prejudice) dramatically played in my mind. Standing at the arrivals gate were the men in the organization who had been blocking me one way or the other, for a very long time. When they saw me with Gurudev, their mouths dropped open in surprise, but I kept walking as though nothing was amiss.

That evening, we all had a good heart-to-heart discussion to talk about how we could collaborate for the good of the organization, going forward. Satisfied that we'd risen above our differences and found common ground, we requested a meeting with Gurudev to work out the details. He, on the other hand, avoided us. No one had a clue as to what would happen next and, knowing his style by now, my bet was on a surprise finish.

Sure enough, just before Gurudev was to leave for the airport, I was called into a private meeting room where a few of our top leaders were gathered. When Gurudev suggested several programs that I should be teaching, the president's newly found goodwill flew right out the window. I listened without saying a word as he put me down and did his best to prevent me from teaching other programs. After a while, when things became overly contentious, I spoke up for myself with power and conviction. Perhaps this was exactly what Gurudev was waiting for—no longer a victim, I was able to address the situation with skill, rising above emotion.

When I finished what I had to say, the room fell silent. A moment later, I was honored when Gurudev appointed me as the first Western teacher for our most powerful personal transformation workshop.

These types of small conflicts and subtle power plays are an everyday part of being in this world. And every time

I did some self-reflection, looking at my own contribution in a conflict, the situation seemed to resolve itself faster, with more grace and peace of mind. The president and I vacillated between getting along one minute and fighting the next, but as yogis, we both knew that we would continue working together until we worked it out...but not before a few broken bones.

The night before my fiftieth birthday, I was in Portland, Oregon, with Gurudev, before we continued on to celebrate Guru Purnima in California. Gurudev was leading a new form of yoga in a completely packed hall where space was so limited that I couldn't stretch my arm out fully without touching the person next to me. I was back on friendly terms with our president, who was also traveling with the Guru. When Gurudev saw us from the stage over-dramatizing the yoga positions for laughs, he led us into a posture that required us to stretch out our arms and to create circles in the air. To be silly, my colleague made the circles super-fast, and as he completed the *asana*, without looking behind him, the full force of his fist landed right on the bridge of my nose. I saw stars and hit the floor in pain while he stood there, his mouth wide open in shock. He felt terrible about what had happened and suggested that we sit together on the flight, but I chose to stay to myself with an ice pack on my nose.

The next morning, a friend who is a physician, recommended I go to the emergency room, which I really didn't want to do since the worst of the pain had subsided.

Instead, I went to meet Gurudev for my birthday. When I told him that I thought our president may have broken my nose during yoga, he just laughed and laughed before lightly touching my nose in three places.

When I finally met with a doctor back in Denver, during the examination she kept repeating, "It isn't medically possible. It isn't medically possible."

I asked, "What isn't medically possible?" It turned out that while my nose was fractured in three places, my severely deviated septum was now virtually perfectly aligned, which she explained just wasn't medically possible without surgery. She didn't want to disturb what had mysteriously happened, but recommended surgery anyway to address the fractures.

Before continuing, I decided to take a chance.

"I have a Guru and when I told him I thought my nose was broken, he touched it in three places. I thought it was odd at first, *Why did he touch it in three places?* Now you tell me my nose was fractured in three places, and you say that my deviated septum is now close to perfect, which is interesting from a meditative perspective. You see, when the air flow is dominant in the left nostril, it's the ideal time for meditation."

The doctor was quiet for a moment before speaking. "Well, Patti, all I can say is that you're a very lucky woman." She scheduled the surgery to smooth down the cartilage to prevent it from becoming any bigger through the years.

I've been active in sports my entire life, from playing kickball as a kid, to waterskiing, snow-skiing, hiking 14,000-foot mountains and playing polo, and I've never broken a bone or required as much as a single stitch. Yet, within one week of turning fifty, my nose was broken, and the following week, while teaching a workshop at our Canadian Ashram, I sprained my ankle. It was clear that turning fifty meant I was about to burn through a lot of karma—quickly.

treadmill **knowledge**

In spite of doing my best to live the knowledge, I still found myself in one frustrating situation after another, for many years. One day I spoke with Gurudev about the repetitive pattern in my life. "You're blossoming so much. So much has been done in your blossoming. It's all in your mind! I want you to be joyful, enthusiastic, happy!" He wasn't the only one.

That evening during *satsang*, he gave a powerful knowledge session, and like people often do, I felt he was speaking directly to me. *"Don't assert your righteousness,"* he said. *"Throw light on the wisdom from within. Don't be stingy with your intellect—use it! Put the talents you have to good use. If you have good speech, use it to do good, not to speak about others. If you're a singer, sing to the Divine. You may be right in one way, but you'll be wrong in another. In silence, there is action; in action, there is silence."*

As he left the hall, he stopped and said to me, "Good *satsang*, Patti?" which I knew meant, "Were you listening? This was for you."

The next day, instead of being with Gurudev and enjoying the afternoon meditations, I was in a training class. Resigned to the present moment, I held a little hope that I might be able to join him at the lake that evening, after class. During the summer, some evenings, Gurudev will take a few people for a ride on the swan boat. Floating on the lake with the Guru and a small group of devotees under a canopy of stars and the light of the moon while a flute plays in the distance always makes me think of the stories I'd read about Krishna in Vrindavan.

To my disappointment, the class continued late into the night. To add insult to injury, one person after another stopped me on the road the next morning to tell me that Gurudev had been looking to take me on the swan boat for my birthday. As I walked into his *kutir*, he started some good-natured teasing. "The biggest security breach has just taken place at the Ashram! You know when anyone in Art of Living hears the name, Patti Montella, they just shake!"

"Well they should!" I retorted, laughing with everyone else, finally free of one big *hot* button.

The next afternoon a few of us were in Gurudev's *kutir*, discussing some business matters. Still dealing with the politics within the organization, and my most prominent nemesis, I made an offhand comment about someone who wanted to become a teacher being mentally unstable. "He's a man and he's crazy...well, he'll probably be the next president of the Art of Living," I said under my breath, unaware that anyone could hear me, until Gurudev started laughing.

Let go and be free.

It's a natural tendency of every human being to want to be free. Freedom is not running away from situations and circumstances. If you are against someone, you have no freedom from them.

Sometimes a situation is stifling or unpleasant, and we run away from it and think this is what freedom is, but that is not so. Anything that stifles you and makes you feel small, being free from that, is what freedom is. Freedom is being un-phased by circumstances, situations and the people around you. Whether you accept it or not, watch it or not, life is an act of letting go. When you feel free from all the cravings and aversions, that is freedom.

—Sri Sri Ravi Shankar

We continued on to Connecticut to celebrate Guru Purnima and later that week, Gurudev called me into a meeting with a few of our leaders, and true to form, the chauvinistic and hostile behavior ensued. I left the room,

seething. Before going to bed that evening, I laid everything at the feet of the Divine and prayed for guidance.

At the gym the next morning, to my surprise Gurudev
walked in. Smiling, I said nothing and continued jogging
on the treadmill, so as not to disturb his workout. He,
however, had another plan in mind. "Why is it that the
DSN teacher is always in the hot seat lately?"

"Because you're her teacher?" I quipped lightly.

Still jogging, Gurudev gifted me with both knowledge
and a blessing. "From now on, you keep silent, no matter what foolishness comes out of a person's mouth. You
change; don't expect anyone else to change. Remember
that the greatest *tapas* (penance) is to bear the ignorance
of a fool. I want you to be free; in fact, you are free right
now!" he declared.

Like an arrow in the hand of a truly skilled archer, once
again, the Guru's wisdom awoke the valor in me. "I take
the challenge, Gurudev. I am already successful!"

"You should respond to an insult with a smile. One with
true patience and courage can respond to any insult or
criticism with an unshakeable smile. And then, chuckling,
he added, "Treadmill Knowledge!"

the year of **yes!**

The first time I heard Gurudev say, "Yes brings peace; no brings conflict," I took the word "Yes" as my own personal mantra for the next year. This is how I ended up living in the Middle East for six months.

A wealthy and devoted couple from Dubai had a vision to develop a high-end spa for women in the most affluent area of Dubai. They requested Gurudev to provide them with a full-time Western teacher to deliver our workshops at the spa, for at least half a year. The idea was that not only would our programs generate more happiness—offering workshops in an environment that locals were familiar with and frequented—would allow us to reach more people.

International assignments are only given to the most senior teachers who are appointed by the Guru. There were whispers that he might assign me, but I wasn't so sure about that, especially as the offer sounded too good to be true. Supposedly the teacher would receive a market value salary, a luxury apartment and the help of a publicist.

When he did offer me the post, I had no choice but to say yes, which may have been surprising since I normally ask a lot of questions when contemplating such a commitment.

"Patti, it's six months. Are you sure?" Gurudev inquired.

"Yes, I'm sure. I will go, but I'll need some education about the culture, so that I don't offend anyone or create an international incident!"

"Just be your natural self," he replied.

Now it was my time to cast a little doubt, "Are you *sure?*" He just smiled.

I accepted the assignment in spite of the fact that I didn't have a clue what I was getting myself into. It took a while for all the logistics to be put into place, and moving on faith, I flew to the United Arab Emirates on Christmas Day.

Landing in the Dubai airport was surreal; I didn't expect to see an enormous Christmas tree, fully decorated with blinking lights, in a Muslim country. Customs was quick and efficient, and thirty minutes later, I was walking out of the airport into the arid desert climate to begin a brand new chapter of life.

I'd always been intrigued by the old movies I'd grown up with, that took place in exotic locations throughout the Middle East. And in spite of all my international travel, this was my first time visiting this part of the world. In preparation for the assignment, I'd read some books about the Emirati culture. While I wasn't required to wear the *abaya* (a long black robe) with a *hijab* (the head-scarf which covers the neck and part of the head), typically worn by UAE women, I did adjust my wardrobe slightly, to be respectful and to draw less attention to myself, as a woman traveling alone.

Dubai is one of the most visited destinations in the world. While it's a cosmopolitan city, it continues to maintain its ancient culture which the government, understandably, expects visitors to respect.

My first night, I was dropped off at the home of a lovely family, where I assumed I would be staying until the apartment was ready. When I learned that they had only planned to host me for one evening, things got complicated. It turned out that the company Gurudev had sent me to work with wasn't established. There was no budget, no PR firm in place, no business plan and no place to live. Thankfully, my hosts graciously agreed to house me for a month until something long term worked out.

Normally, when a teacher is sent on an international assignment, courses are organized in advance. After a week when I hadn't received a single phone call from a local teacher, I spoke with the people who had invited me. Not only had they not made any arrangements for me to teach, it turned out that they actually wanted me to establish a company and learn the spa business. I, in turn, made it clear what my role was; I am a spiritual teacher and I was not in the UAE to start a spa business. When nothing shifted after another week, and with no visible support on the horizon, I made a call to Gurudev. He confirmed my role to those concerned and added that if I was uncomfortable, I should return home.

The spiritual warrior in me woke up; I was not going to accept defeat so early in the game. I made a call to the most senior teacher in the city and invited myself to tea. Over some of the best chai I've ever sipped, I gained clarity on the situation and made a lifelong friend.

I almost fell off of my chair from laughing when she explained what was going on behind the scenes. Apparently, our volunteers mistakenly thought I was there to start a business and make a lot of money. Once I explained the reality of my situation, everything shifted for the better.

My new friend and I attended *satsang* together that evening and I was overjoyed to meet the whole Art of Living Dubai family. It was a sweet reprieve in the midst of all the chaos, but the Divine wasn't anywhere near done with me just yet. In fact, nowhere to stay and no support was just its opening act!

As I was leaving *satsang*, the man who had invited me to the UAE stopped our car. It turned out my temporary host family was going through a personal situation and requested I move out—by the next morning.

My friend assured me that not only would she would find a place for me, but from now on we'd work together to move things forward. The next day, I moved into a luxury apartment at the Dubai Marina, but before I could unpack, I got some more news: I could stay for one week. After that, I had to find another place to live.

Moving on faith, I started organizing speaking engagements for myself and networking. With only two nights left at the apartment and no budget for a hotel, I offered up a prayer.

That evening, a very nice couple with our foundation whom I had never met, called. They wanted to take me out anywhere I'd like to go in Dubai. As a horse lover, I was eager to visit the Dubai Polo Club and arrangements were quickly made for the next day. Just before we hung up the phone, both Tony and Vonita said that it would be their honor if I would consider staying at their home throughout the rest of my time in the UAE. My prayer was answered! The next day, along with their two adorable daughters, we loaded my suitcases into the car and became lifelong friends. When I walked into the room they'd prepared for me, tears came to my eyes. So much love and care had gone into making everything so beautiful and welcoming. I was finally home.

I flew to Kuwait to teach and it didn't take long to realize how different life was in this part of the Middle East. A Western woman traveling alone is not a common sight in this part of the world, and I endured a lot of stares when

I first took a seat on the plane. The woman sitting next to me, in a maid's uniform, starting speaking fast and furiously in Arabic, before another helper in the family exchanged seats with her. The seat switching went back and forth among various family members until the flight attendant finally reaccommodated the family, who was clearly distraught about sitting next to me. Taking it all in stride, I stretched out, grateful for the extra leg room!

The moment I deplaned in Kuwait, the flash and friendliness of Dubai was replaced with dark colors and very little eye contact.

I was the first Western woman to teach our personal transformation program (DSN) in Kuwait, which was scheduled to start the next day. When I learned that the Kuwait police might stop anyone who is on the road late at night, I adjusted our course timings. I was also informed that the police may be watching us, which was unsettling. To be on the safe side, we covered the rented hall windows with curtains, so as not to draw any unnecessary attention to ourselves.

The first night of the course, just as it is anywhere I teach in the world, I immediately connected at the heart level with my students as they unburdened painful memories and stress.

Kuwait is known for its toxic air pollution due to the oil refineries. Like many mothers in Kuwait, one of my students had lost her infant child to a chest infection. Seven years later, her family still blamed her for the child's death and she was miserable. I held her in my arms as she finally released years of grief, shame and guilt. It takes courage for some people to speak freely about what is heavy on their heart, and for some of the men on the course, it took a little time to let go. One man from the course saw me off at the airport, and whispered to me, "I am grateful, Mother."

A few days after returning to Dubai, Vonita had to take me to the emergency room. I was very ill with extreme flu-like symptoms and the doctor informed me that I had "Kuwait Syndrome," a local reference to a complex respiratory illness as a result of air pollution. It was the first but not the last time I would encounter this awful illness, which laid the groundwork for more serious respiratory issues to come. I eventually recovered, and the next month I returned to Kuwait to teach a Happiness course for several hundred people, representing twenty-six countries. It was the largest and most diverse course the chapter had ever organized, and everyone was excited.

Once again, however, we faced a wrinkle in the logistics just before the course began. Again, the organizers didn't want to draw any unnecessary police attention, so we shifted to a location that offered more privacy. With more room to spread out, we were able to arrange proper course seating according to the local custom of separating men and women. With so many countries present, we needed translation. A dedicated team searched the city and we all breathed a sigh of relief when a box arrived filled with translation headsets. As soon as I took the stage, I realized that in all the preparations, I'd never considered how I would be able to tell if the women, most of who were veiled, were connecting with what I was sharing. Typically, when teaching a program about happiness, the student's smile is a sign that the message was received.

But love knows no boundaries, and in a few minutes our eyes did all the talking, soul to soul.

Since the course would run over the dinner hour, we had suggested everyone bring a snack. I was concerned when I saw people eating candy bars for dinner, in a country with a very high rate of diabetes. I requested our volunteers prepare some food for the next day and little did I know just how complicated the task was. Back home, the grocery store shelves are lined with stacks of choices, which is not the case in Kuwait. Inspired by what was taking place on this course, a team of stay-at-home moms organized themselves as efficiently as any military unit, in less than twenty-four hours.

The next evening, 300 healthy and tasty sandwiches were wrapped and piled high on a table. It was fun to see the surprise on the students' faces as they entered the room. During the dinner break, I watched in wonder as men and women gathered around the table together to enjoy the food and one another's company. The doctors on the course approached me on the last night requesting any research we had on the *Sudarshan Kriya*. They'd been monitoring their patients who had diabetes and were amazed to see their blood sugar levels decreasing with the very first breathing technique.

Just before I left Kuwait, I spoke with Rishiji, who is like a brother to me. We hadn't seen one another for several years, and he invited me to meet him in London for a few days. Travel between Dubai and London is popular, which made me think (incorrectly) that it wasn't a big deal to leave my international assignment to travel to another country. I was annoyed that I hadn't been able to reach Gurudev for many months and I was eager for a change of scenery. These are the things my mind used to justify leaving. So when my upcoming courses in Dubai canceled, I booked a flight to London.

The very next day, I was in London and walking into a meditation course Rishiji was teaching. What I had completely forgotten about was that I had taught a course in London just a few years earlier. At least half the people present knew me, which meant, as the saying goes, "The cat was out of the bag." Later that evening, Gurudev called Rishiji. When he called a second time, I started feeling uneasy.

"Patti, do you know what Gurudev asked me?" Rishiji asked. "He asked if I was in London and if you were with me and asked me to give you a message."

"Am I in trouble?" I asked with a slight feeling of trepidation.

"No, but did you really think he wouldn't know where you are or what you're up to, especially when you're working out of the country? The *Guru tattva* (energy) is always with you."

A week later, I was traveling in a large SUV on my way to meet the royal ruling family of Abu Dhabi. My driver, a local Emirati, was doing his best to teach me the UAE national anthem, which was a consolation prize after I refused to bring him back to the States with me.

The evening before, I'd stayed at the home of an Emirati woman I'd become friendly with, who had taken the Happiness course. Sheikh Nahyan bin Mubarak Al Nahyan of Abu Dhabi was a close friend of her family and she had invited me to meet him and to tell him about the work of the Art of Living Foundation in the United Arab Emirates.

Dr Fawzia.

I'll never forget the lavish breakfast my friend and her family had prepared for me. Uncertain of my dietary preferences, the table was filled with all kinds of food, ranging from fresh olives from Palestine to Krispy Kreme donuts and everything imaginable in between. I enjoyed my time with the family, playing with the children and learning about one another's cultures. Before we departed, when we exchanged gifts, they presented me with a traditional Arabian caftan and homegrown dates from their farm.

Our car pulled up to the palace of Sheikh Nahyan who was the Minister of Culture, Youth and Social Development at the time. The moment we stepped into the enormous meeting room, men in traditional Emirati palace uniforms stood on either side of a very long red carpet to officially welcome us. Standing at the end of the carpet, in front of three large ornate wooden chairs, was the Sheikh. As my friend made the introductions, I presented gifts from our Ashram in India and was instructed to sit in one of the three chairs.

As we talked, a young man poured me a small cup of Arabic coffee, a traditional sign of hospitality. I respectfully drank the coffee and placed the cup back onto the tray. The moment I did so, he filled it right back up again. I had no choice but to drink a second cup of the strong and bitter brew. Unsure of how to end this game, my friend caught my eye and signaled to me to shake the cup back and forth, bringing the coffee to an end.

Years later, I saw Sheikh Nahyan once again but from a distance. He was sitting with Gurudev and the Prime Minister of India during the opening ceremony of our World Cultural Festival in Delhi, India. In 2018, Gurudev sent me back to the Middle East to teach for another six months and later that same year, he visited the UAE for the first time, upon invitation of the royal family of Fujairah. After leading meditation and wisdom programs for thousands of people over four days, his tour concluded in the capital city of Abu Dhabi, where he was received at the palace of Sheikh Nahyan, who is now the UAE Minister of Tolerance.

Spiritual teachers scatter the seeds of knowledge, never quite knowing when they will sprout. Yet with a little watering and care, they eventually push up through the soil toward the light.

Jordan was next on my agenda and the moment I arrived, I felt at home driving along the airport road dotted with tall pine trees. That evening, I gave a talk at our local center. Afterward, a woman speaking excitedly in Arabic, hugged me as someone translated. She was very happy about taking a course with me, since she had never met a woman who traveled the world alone or who taught this kind of wisdom. Kissing me on both cheeks, she said she was counting the hours until the program began. The next day, just before class started, she set down a large container on a table next to my chair that she had prepared for me at home. "Don't touch that!" whispered my assistant. "It's Arabic coffee; you'll be up all night!"

260 • becoming unshakeable

This woman's transformation during the course was mind-blowing. She started out in the back of the classroom, but every day she moved closer to the stage and asked more and more questions. Her culture doesn't allow her to travel unescorted, but she was so determined to attend this course that her husband finally relented. He gave her permission not only to come and go on her own each day but to arrive home late at night while he took care of the children.

The class organized an introductory seminar for several hundred people. To this day, I don't know how she did it, but in less than twenty-four hours, she showed up with at least fifty Syrian refugees. It didn't take long to see that she was a natural born leader. Every day, with great enthusiasm, she invited me to her home. I didn't know where I would find the time, but she persisted. Late one night, I was able to make it to their home, located in the oldest area of *Amman*.

I was humbled when I entered the tiny apartment. The children were still dressed in their finest clothes and the small folding table in their living room was buckling from the weight of all the food on top of it. She had been cooking since the morning making hand-rolled grape leaves, bowls of hummus, huge platters of rice and lentils, fresh baked bread and several desserts. As refugees, the family lived on a very modest income, and when her husband complained about how much food she was preparing she quipped back, "Just be glad she's a vegetarian!"

Under a plastic neon-lit picture of Mecca, I listened intently to their story of escaping the state induced terrorism in Syria, with just the clothes on their back. The family continued to live in fear of the government forcing them to return to the nightmare their mother country had become. She told me how renewed and hopeful for the future she was, after attending the course and wanted to know how to share what she'd learned with her fellow refugees. I wanted to see her become a teacher for one of our free programs, which she immediately agreed to do—if her husband would give her permission to do so. While the other women and I cleared the dishes, my male colleague spoke with her husband, who gave his approval and agreed to support her.

The last leg of my journey took me to Muscat, Oman. While the rhythm, traditions and clothing in Oman are unique, the one constant in every Islamic country is the call to prayer five times a day.

The first time I heard the call to prayer was at a local home in Abu Dhabi. I had only been in the country a week when I was invited to meet the family of a new friend. Her brother, a highly educated and successful businessman, wanted to know more about Sri Sri Ravi Shankar and how I had come to the Art of Living foundation. I was in the middle of my story when I heard the call to prayer from the loudspeaker of a nearby mosque. Worried that I may have unintentionally insulted the family by speaking during the call to prayer, I apologized and stopped mid-sentence.

But the family insisted, and although it felt awkward to continue, I learned something very interesting. My hosts explained that according to Islam, if someone is speaking when the call to prayer begins, they are speaking truth. As a result, I was immediately accepted as one of the family.

I stayed in Muscat at the home of a royal family. The Princess was a lovely woman, originally from America and had taken the Happiness course. Every country in the Middle East has its own unique appeal and the sight of the palace, at the top of a mountain offered a breathtaking view of the capital city surrounded by the Al Hajar Mountains and the Arabian Sea.

My course was beginning in a few hours, so I quickly freshened up and made my way to the dining room for a late lunch with an eclectic group of people. Seated at the table was the Princess, an eccentric artist whose husband was conducting research somewhere in Africa, a government official in the traditional clothing which included a cane that kept falling to the floor every few minutes, and myself. The Sultan was in very ill health and couldn't join us.

The Princess was kind enough to accommodate me in the main home, still it took some getting used to the environment. The first evening when I returned from teaching, there was a shot-gun propped up against my door. Perhaps the princes were having a little fun with me; I'll never know. Needless to say, I was grateful when it disappeared the next morning as mysteriously as it had arrived.

That night, I decided it was time to return to the States and called Gurudev. He invited me to attend a discourse he was giving on the Bhagavad Gita, in Arosa, Switzerland. After that, I could return home.

As soon as I landed in Europe, I became aware of how transformative the tour had been. I felt as though I'd been on a six-month silence course and I didn't feel like speaking. I met my dear friend Tanuja at the airport and together, we continued on to Arosa. To my surprise, arrangements had been made for us to room together in the same hotel where Gurudev and his entourage were staying. We immediately opened the windows to soak up the beauty of the Swiss Alps and to breathe in the cool fresh air. After meditating, we set out to find Gurudev. He was with a group of devotees in a small theatre watching the movie Avatar, which was being touted as a cinematic masterpiece with spiritual overtones. Not too long into the movie, Gurudev commented about one of the scenes, noting that it could never happen this way spiritually. He turned to me and said, "People *like* this?" just before ending the evening.

The next morning, I joined him for a walk in the mountains. We trekked up the Swiss Alps in silence until he gently inquired about my

Arosa.

journey. I had no doubt that his question was about much more than my flight from Dubai to Frankfurt. I chose my words carefully. "It was exotic, challenging, and spiritually expanding. But there were many obstacles and should I return to the Middle East again, it might be good to discuss what could be done."

He stopped walking to look at me and simply said, "The obstacles bring out all the skills and talents in you. It brings the *siddhis*. It is good."

ego dissolves **in love**

I once asked one of our Swamis when he thought walking the spiritual path might become easier for me. "My dear, it will never get easier; you're in the Ph.D. program of spirituality—it will only become more difficult as you take more and more responsibility for the welfare of others. The only change will be how you manage your state of mind." He certainly knew what he was talking about.

When I returned to Denver, not only had I changed, but the dynamics in our local chapter had changed as well. Prior to leaving the country, I'd given the green light to our Board, for our fairly new volunteer team to organize a tour for Gurudev, in my absence. I didn't want the volunteers to miss out on a visit from Gurudev and offered to be on call while I was away, as needed. They did a great job, and riding the high that always flows after an event with

Gurudev, two of the leads decided they could do a much better job without me. So much so, that they not only did their best to kick me out of my job, they wanted to see me leave the state altogether.

There are politics everywhere, from where we live and work all the way up to the highest religious institutions in the world. With this in mind, I offered to meet with these two people in an effort to understand their perspective and to find a way to move forward together. Unfortunately, neither had what it took to face me in person.

While I'd been abroad, my old habits and patterns had been replaced with greater confidence, faith, compassion and love. Knowing better than to go down the path of misery, I pulled out my well-worn copy of Gurudev's discourse on the Ashtavakra Gita. The book opened to the chapter, "Ego Dissolves in Love," and the same wisdom that I'd heard and read several times before struck me like never before:

When the mind dies, love dawns. That is why love always brings pain with it—and this dissolving is painful. And so lovers rebel. The mind does not want to dissolve. It wants to emphasize its existence. It wants to show, "I'm something too!" and it doesn't want to bear the pain. In order to get rid of the pain it rebels, and that rebellion is the fight. Let the limited ego dissolve in the Universal ego.

Reflecting on the wisdom, I realized that in the past, not only had I wanted credit for the work I did, I had also wasted a lot of energy trying to control things that were never in my control. I didn't want to be stuck in ego; I'd learned so much wisdom by now. So when Gurudev agreed to return to Denver the next year, I kept this knowledge in mind and did my best to apply it, no matter what came my way. The event was a success and when it was over, I knew that once again, it was time to move on.

the best form
of forgiveness

The following year I was in Chicago to celebrate *Diwali*, the Hindu festival of lights, with Gurudev and thousands of devotees from all over the country. *Diwali* symbolizes spiritual victory of light over darkness, good over evil and knowledge over ignorance. It's a time to remember that every aspect of our life needs our attention and the light of wisdom, and to feel a sense of abundance that the Divine, or nature, is taking care.

Entering the hotel where the event was taking place, I had no idea about the gift nature was sending my way.

I was sharing a room with two of my students and was eager to connect with them. They had taken a personal transformation course with me years earlier where they'd finally let go and started living life authentically. As a result, we'd formed a strong bond, and I'd been coaching them on the path ever since. This was the first course that they'd taken the lead on as organizers, and it was time to celebrate. But when I saw them in the hotel lobby, they looked anything but happy. Unsure of what was going on, we rode the elevator to our room. As key volunteers, they had been able to reserve a room on the same floor with Gurudev and his entourage.

The elevator doors opened and we were greeted by the main event organizers. They were sitting at a desk making sure that everyone entering had an actual room on that floor, something I'd never encountered. On one hand, this couple did a lot of service, but on the other hand they had earned a reputation as being untruthful and manipulative organizers who created all kinds of trouble whenever they were in charge. With strained smiles, we showed them our room keys.

My students were visibly uncomfortable, and as soon as we were alone I pushed for an explanation. With tears in their eyes they explained that at first, this couple had refused to give them a room anywhere near Gurudev's suite simply because I was staying with them. A big drama had ensued, and in the end, we were allowed to have a room on the same floor as Gurudev, as long as it was as far away from his meeting space and suite as possible. The couple had gone as far as to make up a lie that Gurudev himself had told them that I was not to be placed anywhere near his floor. I could see the seed of doubt about me in my students' faces from this outrageous lie. Such blatant slander had the potential to destroy my good name and livelihood and I felt my fire rising, which I'd have to deal with later. For now, it was imperative that I remain steady for the sake of my students. I reassured them that all was well and that this was just another misguided ploy by this couple to control who was around the Guru, in order to keep him to themselves. They were greedy for his attention and blinded by the illusion of power. My students felt better after we spoke and left to take care of a few things.

For so many years walking this path toward enlightenment, I'd faced one health challenge after another while enduring my fair share of sabotage, criticism, chauvinism, and injustice. All the while, the Guru Mandala was pulling at me, but with the grace of the Guru and my own determination to realize something greater than myself, I had been able to stay in knowledge and keep moving forward in spite of the dark nights of the soul that filled me with doubts. But this time felt like one battle too many, and I broke down crying, feeling defeated.

So, while everyone was at the event, I took a taxi to a different hotel. I was at a tipping point and needed some time away from everyone and everything to figure things out.

When I was a no-show at the celebration, a friend called to find out where I was. I explained what had happened and how upset I was. Later that evening, Gurudev's secretariat also called to find out what had happened and where I was, I assume on Gurudev's instruction since he'd been informed about what was going on. He did his best to convince me to return to the hotel and to talk things out, but he definitely wasn't the person I needed to speak with. I cried throughout the night, my mind filled with doubts about whether or not I wanted to continue.

Forgiving others with a sense of compassion is the best form of forgiveness.

Inside every culprit, there is a victim crying for help. When you see from a wide-angle lens, you see that a culprit is also a victim. When you see that victim inside the culprit, you don't need to forgive. Forgiveness happens; in fact, compassion spontaneously arises in your heart. The highest form of forgiveness is realizing that the other committed a mistake out of ignorance and having a sense of compassion for them. Cultivating this sense of forgiveness in oneself is a mark of being noble in character.

—Sri Sri Ravi Shankar

After my morning *sādhanā*, with my mind and emotions more settled, my perception shifted. Most people give up just short of the summit; I was not going to be one of those people. The best view is always at the top and I intended to make it; I wanted total freedom, total equanimity, this lifetime. For the second time in twenty-four hours, I packed up my suitcase and returned to the city. By now, the hotel was bursting at the seams with Art of Living members. Still a bit fragile, I kept my head down and went to find the one person who would shine the light of wisdom on the situation, so that I could reach the summit.

Gurudev gently let me know that I had been missed, saying nothing about the situation from the day before. In the expansive space of meditation and *satsang*, I returned to my center. The next day, when I ran into the man who had created all the trouble, it was evident that he'd been chastised for his behavior because he couldn't even look at me. I almost felt sorry for him but then reminded myself of all the cruel things he had done or said through the years and kept on walking.

The night before Gurudev was leaving, he called me into his meeting room to talk about what had happened.

"What were you thinking, leaving the hotel like that? You didn't even speak to anyone about what was happening."

"No one knew I left, Gurudev."

He cautioned me not to get into defense consciousness. "Because you are in the knowledge and know better, this karma is now on you. Where was your faith in the Divine to take care? The Divine would have taken care. From now on, you will have compassion in the face of ignorance, come what may. Write this down. Never forget it again."

While I was shocked by his words, I also noticed something stirring in my consciousness. I'd known many stories of Gurudev being mistreated by people who were jealous of him and who wished him ill will for one igno-rant reason or another. He'd endured slanderous accusa-tions, blame, and even death threats—yet never had I seen him move in any manner other than total peace and equa-nimity. His infinite compassion in the face of ignorance changes millions of lives every day, and now he expected me to follow in his footsteps, which meant it was possible.

I bowed in gratitude for the power of his intention and the profound lesson.

The next morning, the traditional arti ritual, in rever-ence of the one who brings love and light, was performed for Gurudev. One of the ladies was shy, and as she circled Gurudev with the candle, her hands shook so much that she almost singed his eyebrows! Gurudev laughed and moved away from the fire just before playfully rolling his eyes back and forth to see if he still had eyebrows.

So much had shifted within me through this latest experience, and I was eager to speak with Gurudev about it. As we took the elevator to the meditation hall together, I took my chance. "I'm the happiest person in the world for getting a scolding! I feel incredibly free. I'm posi-tive that some big impression is gone now. Thank you, Gurudev, from the bottom of my heart." He smiled, gave me a thumbs up and the elevator doors opened. In a flash, he was engulfed by thousands of enthusiastic devotees.

Later that day, the man who had created all the trouble started apologizing when he saw me, but I stopped him. What had happened was in the past and it was obvious that he was aware of his mistake. Instead of giving him a hard time about what he'd done, I praised him for his work in organizing our event.

Years later, I shook my head in disbelief when I came across the tweet that Gurudev sent on that same night: "Light the lamp of knowledge to dispel ignorance. Light the lamp of knowledge to dispel cruelty. Happy *Diwali*." The gift of knowledge had apparently been on its way from the very start.

life is a **game**

There are four pillars of knowledge: Discrimination, Dispassion, the Six Wealths and the Desire for Freedom (Moksha). I've been listening to and applying this wisdom ever since I stepped foot on this path. Through the years I'd been able to move beyond the intellect to an experiential understanding of each pillar. There was just one pillar that wasn't quite as strong as the others—until now.

Many years ago, I had shared my frustration with Gurudev about how slow things were moving in the work we were doing, particularly in the West. I was also a little confused at the time about who I was. One minute I was as American as apple pie and baseball, and the next I was wearing a *saree* and singing in Sanskrit.

It took a long time to finally understand his response, which was: *"You still want something from the world, that's why you have this question. Go deeper into your meditation. Look into death, then you will know who you are. See everyone dead, even me. You will evolve. The answer will come to you and you will have fulfillment. Like the sun, it just gives its rays, whether someone takes them or not. Then you will realize you are here just to serve, no need for results. Then you will say, thy will be done."*

Dispassion is your strength.

Dispassion or "vairagya" is one of the pillars of the highest knowledge. You should know that dispassion is not apathy; it is simply a broader perspective of reality. Dispassion is moving back home toward the source, which is a reservoir of enthusiasm. Dispassion is lack of feverishness; it gives you a joy that nothing else can give you. Dispassion connects you to the present moment and brings ease in life. Dispassion is the strength in you. When you're centered and calm, you can understand that everyone who has come to this world has come to give something to the world. We have nothing to take from here. Dispassion is what you invoke in yourself.

—Sri Sri Ravi Shankar

I have yet to meet anyone who is as busy, sought after, and as accommodating as Gurudev, in his mission to bring a lasting smile to every face. He receives thousands of requests every day for his guidance on a multitude of issues from people representing every walk of life. It's a mystery how he is able to answer every sincere question and prayer. On any given day, the Ashram in Bangalore feeds almost 20,000 people. Wherever he goes, thousands of people stand in line just to catch a glimpse of him. I feel that I'm one of the most fortunate people on the planet, to have become his student early on.

It's common to forget what you want to say or ask in front of Gurudev. I once brought a scientist with a prestigious university to meet him. Afterward, the scientist who was so proud of his intellect said, "I completely forgot what I was going to say. I felt so blissed out in his presence, nothing came to my mind."

Not too long ago, while traveling with Gurudev, I was eager to get his clarity on a few things and made my usual list of questions. In the early years, he used to tease me about my lists, by saying, "Is the job done? Have we discussed everything on your list?"

Gurudev once told me that the purpose of all questions and all answers is to bring a yes to our consciousness; this is meditation. Nowadays, I have fewer questions and more wonder, and I'm a lot happier! Still, every so often, something comes up that requires his attention. So, as we buckled in, I took out my list. "I'm going to rest on this flight," he said pointing to the small piece of paper with a hint of mischief in his voice.

"I don't think there will be any rest on this short flight, Gurudev. It's only forty minutes and I've been waiting a long time to go over a few things." He opened a bag of potato chips and handed it to me. "Here, eat this!" he joked, as if potato chips could stop me from talking to him! By the time we landed, I was very grateful that he had time to meditate and I had a few answers. But he wasn't done with the teasing. At the arrivals gate, a devotee asked him how his flight was. "Have you seen the movie *Life of Pi* about being stranded for six months with a Bengal tiger? It was like that!" I laughed right along with everyone else at the joke.

The more the witness consciousness grows in you, the more playful and unshakeable you become.

Whatever the challenges, we need to keep making efforts to create a better world. This is possible when we are established within ourselves. In you, there is an actor and there is a witness. The actor is either confused or decisive, but the witness just observes and smiles. As you go inward, the witness aspect grows in you and you remain untouched by events. And as you go outward, the actor in you becomes more skillful in responding to situations. The more the witness grows in you, the more playful and unshakeable you become. Then trust, faith, love, and joy all manifest in and around you. These two entirely opposite aspects of our being are nurtured by meditation.

—Sri Sri Ravi Shankar

I was not the person I had started out as, when I embarked on this spiritual path. I no longer took life so seriously and could laugh at myself; I'd learned to take life as the game that it is.

Boone, North Carolina.

reborn at **sixty**

Just before my sixtieth birthday, Gurudev sent me back to the Middle East for another tour. Then, just when I was ready to return to the States, he surprised me not once, but twice, by sending me to the Philippines, where terrorism is on the rise in the south. I was grateful to have played a role in helping to foster an agreement between the government and the IAHV, in our mutual effort to offset the recruitment of youth to terrorist regimes. After my second visit, I traveled with Gurudev to India and several other countries in Southeast Asia, attending a number of workshops he led on the *Vigyan Bhairav*. This ancient text offers 112 meditation techniques that can lead to an inner awakening and expanded reality of the self and hasn't been shared on this planet for more than 10,000 years. The course was out of this world.

Gurudev arranged for a special Vedic ceremony to be held at our Canadian Ashram, in honor of my sixtieth birthday. Astrologically, when we turn sixty, all the planets in the zodiac are in the same positions, or occupy the same astrological houses of the zodiac, as they were on the day we were born.

TOP: *Cleveland Clinic, 2017.* BOTTOM:*Philippines, 2018.*

The powerful Vedic ceremony called *Shashtidbdapoorthi* is traditionally conducted for men and I was deeply honored to have it performed on my behalf. The sacred ceremony is intended to nullify our negative karmas while enhancing our positive vibrations. The *yajna* or fire ceremony conducted by Vedic priests signifies a rebirth. The idea of entering the next phase of life with all the blessings possible left me awestruck.

I was excited and nervous for the ceremony to begin. My friends helped me to dress up in a beautiful blue and gold silk *saree* that Bhanu, Gurudev's sister, had gifted me for my birthday. I had no idea what to expect or what I was supposed to do when I walked into the meditation hall, and looked to Gurudev for direction. He smiled and pointed to a small wooden stool in front of the fire, surrounded by the Vedic priests and the numerous items that had been prepared for the ceremony.

A little surprised, I took my seat. Looking over at Gurudev and at everyone gathered, I was overwhelmed with the intensity of love and grace in the room. For the first time, I not only understood how much the Divine cared for me and had been with me every step of the way, I felt it. Wiping away a few tears, I closed my eyes, settled in, and sailed away into the beautiful depth of the Self.

The path of Vedic wisdom is not the road I imagined I would walk or ever thought that I would have the opportunity to walk when I was a little girl. Yet it has turned out to be the right and best path for me—answering a sincere prayer to live life to my highest human potential.

The first thirty years of my life I did my best to project an image of confidence and success to the outside world, and yet, I now have a whole new definition of what success and confidence truly are.

We are so much more than these bodies that provide us temporary housing. We are so much bigger than the doubts that run amok in our minds or the trivial problems that we sometimes allow to consume us. We waste so

60th Birthday Vedic Ceremony.

much valuable time and precious life force energy anytime we look to things outside of ourselves to make us happy.

Whatever traumas, limitations, or misconceptions you may have identified with cannot diminish the beautiful truth of who you are at your core. This is your spiritual essence, and it never ceases to be, like the sun that is always shining even when it's obstructed by clouds. Every storm that has come into your life has widened your horizons, spiritually speaking. It has destroyed what is small within you, and in so doing, given you a deeper understanding of your true greatness. The power to awaken to your own Divine nature is within you, and the access point is as close to you as your own breath.

Through the love and grace of my beloved Guru, and thanks to determination and true grit, I have come to realize something far greater than myself and am blessed to have the opportunity to share this discovery with others.

Today, the questions that raced through my mind all those years ago are silenced. I am unshakeable, my heart is full, and I am at peace.

It turns out that I am the one I was seeking all along. And I venture to say, the same is true for you.

acknowledgments

This book would never have been possible without the love, support, guidance, friendship, and cheerleading efforts of many, many people.

Gurudev, finding you again, was an answer to a sincere pray. Because of your unconditional love, infinite patience, depth of wisdom, boundless joy, and unwavering commitment to the blossoming of my consciousness, I am blessed with unshakeable faith and the ability to move through life with a lasting smile. Words can never express what is in my heart.

Mom and Dad, you wrapped me in a blanket of love and laid a strong foundation that allowed me to discover and live my truth. You had the patience to let me move "to the beat of my own drum," even when it made you want to pull your hair out! You taught me to be a strong woman and to stand up for myself and others. Thank you for always, always being there for me.

Bhanumathi Narasimhan, I am so grateful to call you my friend and to walk this path with you as my spiritual sister. You have always been and continue to be authentic and so generous in sharing your love, wisdom, stories, and teachings so that I, and others, may learn and grow.

Thank you to my family for sticking with me on this journey, even when it didn't make sense, especially my sisters, Joanne Montella-Trcka and Kathy Montella.

DN, thank you for bringing JA into my life. Because of our friendship and what we went through together, I ended up putting both feet on the spiritual path.

Thank you to my first teachers on the path, David Longnecker, Philip Fraser, Dean Harmison and Janael McQueen. We were old friends from the moment we met.

Rishi Nityapragya, Swami Brahmatej, Swami Sadyojathah and Prashant Rajore: Each of you have been a guiding light, a friend and my spiritual brother on this incredible journey.

Michael Sherrod, you have held my hand throughout the entire process of creating this book. Thank you for pushing me to "put myself out there" and to just start writing. Thank you for listening to 1,000-plus ideas that you knew would never go anywhere and still encouraging me to keep on creating! I'm so grateful for our everlasting friendship.

Werner Luedemann and Ewald Poeran, our early days together, when we were just starting IAHV, are incredibly precious memories, as is your friendship. Susannah Rowley, you were an incredible resource as we worked together in building IAHV and taught me how to write a rock-solid press release! Filiz Odabas-Geldiay, from our first days together in Washington, DC, and always—I am grateful for you.

Caroline Zeman, you are in a category all your own. You have been a beloved sister from the start. I can never thank you and Wally Zeman enough for all your love and support. Denise Richardson, you are a diamond among friends and a light to the world; thank you for absolutely everything. Michael Collins, thank you for answering every "SOS" I sent—my Italian Irish brother. Shirley Harmison, Tanuja Limaye, Marcy Jackson and Anne Farrow—our spiritual sisterhood lives on! Michael Fischman, Jeff Houk, and John Osborne, walking this path wouldn't have been the same without each of you.

Danielle Dorman, you are an editor extraordinaire! Writing a book has been a very intimate process; it's a bit like giving birth. I knew from our first phone call that you were just the right person to help me to bring this baby safely into the world.

Kathy Murray and Ann Shamleffer, thank you for giving Checkers, Mia, and I a home when we needed it most. Thank you to everyone who has been kind enough to host me, especially Neelam and Vinod Patel.

I am grateful to all of my students for your love and all I have been able to see and learn through you.

Jai Guru Dev

helpful **references**

To connect with the author and to learn more about the techniques and programs referenced in this book, please visit:

Patricia (Patti) Montella
www.pattimontella.com
Twitter: @PattiMontella
Instagram: pattimontella
Facebook: Patti Montella

The Art of Living Foundation
www.artofliving.org

Research on the *Sudarshan Kriya*™
http://aolresearch.org/

The International Association for Human Values
www.iahv.org

Project Welcome Home Troops
www.pwht.org

about the **author**

Patti Montella has been a pioneer, risk taker, and leader her entire life. She built a thriving career on the cutting-edge of travel technology before leaving it all behind to dedicate her life to uplifting society. The skills she sharpened in the business world have served her well as an international speaker and inner transformation coach who's taught tens of thousands of people worldwide—from CEOs and government leaders to royalty and college students—over the past twenty-five years. Through her work in key leadership roles with the Art of Living Foundation and the International Association for Human Values, Patti has become an internationally recognized happiness expert and a powerful agent of change.

Made in the USA
Columbia, SC
04 November 2019